FOUR CORNERSTONES OF INSPIRATIONAL LEADERSHIP

FROM WAR ROOM TO THE BOARDROOM

COLONEL AJAI LAL

Contents

Preface: Why This Book Matters

A Personal Welcome

Have you ever had a moment when the ground beneath your feet felt uncertain, and everything familiar seemed to pause?

That question isn't theoretical for me. I've lived it. Once, while lying flat on the cold riverbed during a combat operation, unable to move, my right knee was crushed. The mission was complete, but I knew my military career had ended at that exact moment. Years later, I found myself walking into boardrooms across the world. No longer in uniform, but still carrying the same sense of mission. I hadn't studied business in a classroom, but I had lived it in the raw form that tests clarity, discipline, and the ability to bring people together around a goal. Those years in the corporate world didn't replace what I had learned in the military. They sharpened it. They showed me that leadership principles hold true whether you're in fatigues or a tailored suit. And over time, I knew I wanted to pass that on. Coaching didn't come from a need to reinvent. It came from the conviction that what works in war rooms and boardrooms can equip others to lead with greater intent.

If there's one thing I've learned across these chapters of my life, it's this: leadership begins when the façade falls away. What remains is who you are under pressure, what principles you hold on to, and how you carry others through the storm.

My story started early. I am a second-generation army officer who grew up with a passion for the uniform. At fifteen, I joined the National Defence Academy. This decision wasn't based on calculation. It was driven by instinct, pride, and a deep respect for the uniform. Over the next twenty-five years after my training for 4 years, I served in the Indian Army, led operations under fire, commanded my tank regiment, and took on high-risk assignments in some of the world's most volatile regions, including Sri Lanka and post-genocide Cambodia.

Then everything changed on 11 December 1997. That riverbed incident didn't just end my time in uniform. It stripped me of something far more personal, my sense of identity. The accident on my tank during an operational mission ended my time in uniform, but not the years it had shaped me. I was a man facing the kind of silence that follows when everything familiar disappears. The rhythm was broken. The structure I had lived by no longer held. What remained was a stillness I hadn't known before. Pain settled in first, followed by doubt, and then a long stretch of uncertainty that demanded a different kind of strength.

But something else showed up in that silence: a decision. I chose not to give in. I chose to speak my mind rather than obey it. That choice, to lead myself, became the foundation of everything that followed.

With no MBA, no business background, and zero experience in the corporate world, I joined NIIT Ltd., a global talent development corporation. The learning curve was steep, but I relied on what I knew: mission clarity, disciplined action, and leading people by purpose, not position. Over the next fifteen years, I helped drive business across forty countries. We weren't just building systems, we were building futures. Skill development projects in Bhutan, South Africa, the Maldives, China, Latin America, South East Asia, and the African continent gave thousands of young people access to learning, dignity, and jobs. Every initiative had one thing in common: leadership rooted in action.

Now, in this third phase of my life, I work with leaders who are often carrying more than they show. They lead companies, teams, and communities. But many of them are fighting silent battles, unsure of where they stand. Over the past ten years, I've coached more than ten thousand individuals. And what I've come to believe is this: Leadership, at its core, is about inspiring others to reach for more within themselves. It's not rooted in control or authority. It's reflected in how you lift people, how you help them see what they're capable of, and how you guide them to bring that potential forward.

That's what this book is built on.

The ideas I'll share are not theories. They weren't written behind a desk or drawn on a whiteboard. They were shaped through action, failure, and reflection. The framework I use with leaders today has four cornerstones: *passion, people, performance, and legacy.*

Whether you're leading a business or rebuilding yourself after a loss, whether you're in the military, a startup, or somewhere in between, this book is for you. It will challenge you to define what you stand for, how you show up, and what you'll leave behind.

The Genesis of the Four Cornerstones

Some of the clearest lessons I've learned didn't arrive in training rooms or during scheduled reviews. They came unannounced, often when things were falling apart and decisions couldn't wait. That's where leadership reveals itself. And over time, those moments began shaping something I could stand on.

My leadership journey began with the rigor of the military. Early on, we were introduced to the Chetwode Motto. It was more than a slogan carved in stone. It was a code to live by and lead by. The safety, honor, and welfare of the country came first. The men you lead came next. And your own comfort, always last. That order of priority was drilled into us, not through words, but through how we trained, fought, and carried ourselves every day.

Over the years, I had the chance to command soldiers and an armoured regiment in some of the most complex and hostile conditions. Whether it was the volatile regions of Sri Lanka or leading multi-national teams during United Nations missions in Cambodia or commanding an armoured regiment, leadership was tested not by what you said, but by what you did under pressure. When you're guiding teams through unknown terrain, handling ceasefire violations, or briefing diplomats while surrounded by landmines, clarity becomes the only reliable compass.

Later, when I stepped into the business world, I found those same lessons playing out in different ways. Teams needed direction. Culture shaped momentum. Trust either strengthened or broke down the execution. What worked in battle translated seamlessly into boardrooms, once the surface differences were removed.

Then came the work I do now, coaching leaders, many of whom carry weight silently. Some of them are responsible for thousands of employees. Others are leading start-ups, schools, or businesses. But the deeper struggles are often the same. They're not asking for motivation. They're searching for structure, for clarity, and for a way to lead that still feels anchored when things around them keep shifting.

As I coached, I started noticing patterns. No matter the domain, the same four areas kept surfacing. They were there when leadership succeeded, and they were missing when it failed.

That's when I gave them shape.

Passion. People. Performance. Legacy.

These four are not steps. They are anchors. They hold a leader steady when roles change, when expectations rise, and when things begin to stretch.

Passion gives depth to the action. It's the internal fire that keeps you committed long after others lose interest. It's the kind of energy that keeps you moving forward, even when it hurts.

People define the spirit of the team. In the military, it was called morale. In every other setting, it's the same thing in different words. When people feel cared for, they stand stronger. When they don't, even the sharpest strategy fails.

Performance is the act of daring. Not reckless action, but the kind that comes from courage with preparation. When people are supported, they begin to stretch. And when they stretch, they grow.

Legacy is what lasts. It's not a title or a reputation. It's the impact your leadership leaves behind, whether you're there to see it or not.

There's one story that brings all of this into sharp focus for me.

It was 1999. The Kargil War was underway. Captain Vikram Batra and his unit were tasked with capturing Point 5140, one of the most heavily fortified enemy positions. The mountain stood at a steep incline, over seventeen thousand feet in altitude. The climb was nearly vertical. The enemy had the advantage of position, and they were well prepared. But Batra's team moved with speed and resolve. They completed the mission without a single casualty.

After securing the peak, he radioed the success signal. His words were brief. "Yeh Dil Maange More."

He wasn't celebrating. He was ready for the next fight.

Three weeks later, he was handed another mission. This time, it was Point 4875. The objective was critical. The peak overlooked the highway that connected Srinagar to Leh. If the enemy held it, they would have control over the route. Once again, the task came with a brutal climb. Again, the enemy held the higher ground. And again, Batra stepped forward.

What stood out wasn't just his courage. It was the way his team responded. Soldiers from other sections asked to join him in the assault. They didn't want to miss the chance to fight alongside him. That kind of loyalty doesn't come from authority. It comes from trust.

As they neared the top, gunfire intensified. One of his men was hit. Without hesitation, Batra moved toward him. Subedar Raghunath Singh, the soldier's senior, tried to help. Batra stopped him. He said, "You have a family and children. I'm not even married. Main sar ki taraf rahunga, aur aap paanv uthayenge." I'll take the head, you lift his legs.

He crawled forward, exposed to enemy fire, and tried to pull the wounded soldier to safety. He was shot in the chest at close range. A split second later, a splinter hit his head. He collapsed beside the man he was trying to save.

He didn't make it back.

But his team did. And they finished what he started. Point 4875 was captured. The tricolor was hoisted. The mountain is now known as Batra Top.

That story doesn't need embellishment. His actions said everything.

This wasn't a moment built for applause. It wasn't a grand gesture. It was a decision made in a fraction of a second. It came from clarity, conviction, and a deep sense of duty.

That is leadership in its truest form.

When I think about the Four Cornerstones, I don't think of theory. I think of that kind of presence. That kind of purpose. And that kind of courage. Captain Batra didn't talk about passion, people, performance, or legacy. He lived them. Every part of that mission reflected what those words mean when they are real.

He didn't survive the war. But what he left behind will outlast medals and titles. He left behind a standard. And that standard still speaks.

When I look back at my journey, a few questions still guide me.

What do I want to be remembered for? What will people remember about my leadership once I've moved on? What will my legacy be?

Answering those questions brought me to this next chapter of life. I now coach, write, and teach from the same principles that shaped my own path. Over the years, I've come to believe something that has held true across every setting:

Leaders dream more than what others think as practical.

Expect more than what others think as possible.

And care for people more than what others think as wise.

That is the spirit behind the framework I share in this book.

Each chapter ahead will explore one of these four ideas. Not as theory, but through lived experience. These are principles that stand when things are uncertain and keep you grounded when things move fast.

What Will You Gain?

This book is built on what leadership looks like when guessing isn't an option. It comes from years of leading in high-pressure environments, on the field, in unfamiliar markets, and inside organizations where clarity had to cut through complexity. What you'll find here didn't start in theory. It was forged in places where hesitation had consequences and direction had to be clear.

Over the years, I've led a tank regiment in conflict zones, coordinated peacekeeping operations with officers from over thirty nations, scaled businesses in unfamiliar regions, and coached leaders through situations where their choices shaped everything around them. Throughout all of this, one thing kept showing up: When a leader is clear, committed, and deeply invested in their people, things begin to align. Momentum builds, and trust becomes real.

This book gives you a structure to lead from that place.

You'll explore four principles: Passion, People, Performance, and Legacy. Each chapter brings them to life through real stories. These are not polished case studies. They are drawn from moments where leadership was tested, and something true had to emerge. You'll see what strengthens a team and what breaks it. What holds under pressure, and what quietly gives way when it's missing?

You'll also find space to turn the lens inward. At the end of each chapter, there are questions to help you pause and think. They're not there to test you. They're there to bring you back to what matters. What drives you? How do you lead when no one is watching? And what kind of imprint are you leaving behind?

This book is written for people who lead in the real world. Whether you're building a business, commanding a team, managing a classroom, or holding things together at home, the principles still apply. You don't need a title. You need the willingness to act with clarity and purpose.

What you'll read here comes from more than five decades of leading across different worlds. The roles changed. The settings changed. What remained was the need to hold people and outcomes with equal weight, to build trust while demanding excellence, and to listen deeply while setting a clear direction. When leaders bring that balance with consistency and conviction, people respond in ways you can't always measure, but you always feel.

That's what this book offers.

For Whom This Book is Written

This book is meant for leaders at all levels. That doesn't always mean someone in uniform or a corner office. It means anyone who takes responsibility when things get unclear. Anyone who chooses to act when staying passive would find it easier.

You could be starting your leadership journey, trying to figure out what really matters. Or maybe you've been leading for years and are tired of chasing goals that leave you feeling empty. You might be building something new or managing people in a space that feels unpredictable. You might be in the armed forces, in a business, in government, or at the head of a small team that looks to you for direction. If you care about how you show up and how others grow because of it, then this book will speak to you. This book is for leaders. That doesn't always mean someone in uniform or sitting at the top of an organization. It means anyone who takes responsibility when the path ahead isn't clear. Anyone who steps forward when others hesitate. Anyone others looks to when something needs to move and waiting is no longer an option.

You might be stepping into leadership for the first time, still finding your footing. Or you might have years behind you, with plenty of wins and more than a few hard calls. You could be leading in business, in the armed forces, in education, in government, or in a smaller space where your decisions still shape people's lives. If you've ever had to hold the weight of other people's trust, this book has something for you.

My own journey has taken me through the Army, peacekeeping missions, global business, and now coaching. Across all these settings, I've come to see that leadership holds its shape, even when the environment shifts. The pressures change. The language adjusts. What stays constant is the need for clarity, consistency, and truth in how a leader shows up. People respond to someone who is steady in action and sincere in intent, someone who doesn't perform the role but lives it. Authenticity builds that connection. It's what allows trust to grow, even in uncertain moments.

This book is for those who care about how they lead. It's for:

- Those who want to act with clarity, even when things feel chaotic

- Leaders who've seen success but still feel something's missing

- New leaders are trying to grow without losing what matters

- Veterans bringing their values into a new chapter

- Coaches, educators, and mentors who influence others by how they live

What you'll find here didn't come from a classroom. These lessons were lived, tested, and carried through different kinds of work, in different corners of the world. The stories shared are not tied to a title or a setting. They are drawn from moments when someone had to act, and that decision made the difference.

At the heart of all those moments is the same truth: leadership is about people. Their trust. Their effort. Their belief in the person they follow. You don't need a title to earn that. You need to show up with clarity and lead as it matters.

If that's what you're aiming for, then this book is written with you in mind.

How to Use This Book

There are a couple of ways you can read this book. You can move through it from start to finish, the way I've written it. Or you can open it to a section that speaks to something you're currently facing and begin from there. Either approach will help. But if you're looking to absorb the full weight of these ideas and apply them in a connected way, I would suggest starting from the beginning.

Each of the four sections, Passion, People, Performance, and Legacy, stands strong on its own. But it is the connection between them that unlocks something bigger. I've seen that firsthand. In high-stakes military operations and in boardrooms across the world, the shift doesn't come from fixing one part in isolation. It comes when there's alignment across all of them. When a leader is clear on why they are here, focused on how they show up for people, decisive when action is needed, and steady in the way they build their impact, everything starts to move with more power.

That's why this book is laid out the way it is. It's not theory dressed up as advice. It follows a rhythm I've worked with for years in coaching, and more importantly, one I've lived.

If you're picking this up in response to a specific challenge, you're welcome to jump ahead to the section that feels most relevant. There's nothing wrong with that. But I would still encourage you to return to the full sequence when you're ready. You'll see how each area builds on the others, and how a gap in one place often explains what's breaking down somewhere else.

At the end of each chapter, you'll find a set of questions. These are not there to test you. They're there to slow things down, to help you step back and think clearly. If you treat them seriously, they will do what no strategy session can: they'll help you reconnect with your own judgment.

Toward the back of the book, you'll find additional tools I've used with the leaders I coach. You don't need to use them all. But if you're ready to work on something specific, those tools can offer structure when the situation feels unclear.

This book can be read alone, in a group, with your team, or as part of a coaching conversation. However you use it, bring your full self. Bring honesty. Bring the willingness to see things as they are. The rest will follow.

What you're holding is not a theory manual. It's built from the field. It was written to be used, not to be admired.

A Call to Leadership

Over the years, I've come to see one thing with absolute clarity. Leadership is influence. In the military, that influence runs deeper than words. It's what moves soldiers to step forward even when they know the risk. Sometimes, it means inspiring them to make the ultimate sacrifice. That kind of trust isn't built through rank or command alone. It's built through presence, through how a leader carries themselves when it matters most. You can have the authority to decide, to instruct, to manage. But if people don't believe in who you are, the title won't carry you far. The influence shows up in the quiet moments when others hesitate, and you choose to act.

The four cornerstones you're about to explore in this book have one job. They help raise that standard. When these ideas are applied with consistency and clarity, your ability to inspire others grows. And that is what leadership really is. You don't have to change who you are. But you do have to decide how seriously you want to grow in how you lead.

I've seen it across all phases of my life. In military operations where morale became the difference between moving forward and breaking down. In corporate environments where outcomes shifted because someone chose to own their role instead of waiting for instructions. And in coaching rooms where leaders finally made sense of the confusion by returning to what mattered.

These ideas are not limited to crises. They work when things are calm, too. They guide how you make decisions in boardrooms, in classrooms, and in everyday life. They come into play when you're mentoring someone, stepping into a hard conversation, or trying to lead a team that feels stuck.

So let me offer this as clearly as I can. If you're picking up this book, don't skim it. Don't use it for ideas you can quote. Use it to sharpen how you show up. These four principles are not meant to sound good on paper. They are meant to be used. Not all at once. Not in a rush. But with care and commitment, over time.

Whether you're leading a team, a company, a unit, or your own household, this applies to you. It doesn't matter where you're starting. What matters is how far you're willing to go.

The first chapter begins with Passion. I've started there for a reason.

Without passion, nothing holds. You can have the best plan, the strongest talent, and the sharpest strategy. But if you are not anchored by something real inside you, everything begins to slip. Passion is the fire that keeps you going when the work is hard, the results are slow, and the noise around you says give up.

So start there. Read it slowly. Think hard. Then act.

Chapter

01

Passion – The Fire That Drives Leadership

The Power of Passion

Passion is often misunderstood in leadership circles. People confuse it with enthusiasm, energy, or the ability to sound convincing. But real passion doesn't need noise. It isn't about feeling excited. It's about staying committed when everything around you starts to test that commitment.

I've seen passion show up when there was no applause, no recognition, and no visible reward. It came through in quiet decisions made under pressure. It lived in the actions of people who kept going because the mission mattered more than their comfort.

I was fifteen when I stepped into the National Defence Academy. By the time I passed out of the Indian Military Academy, I wasn't chasing glory. What drove me was harder to put into words. It was a sense of duty that settled deep in the gut, something more grounded than pride.

I served for twenty-five years in the military. Led men through terrain most wouldn't walk through on a clear day. I watched them push themselves past exhaustion, fear, and every excuse the mind usually clings to. That kind of resilience doesn't come from adrenaline. It comes from a passion that doesn't fade when the stakes rise.

On 11th December 1997, that idea of passion became personal. I was leading my regiment in a river-crossing exercise near the border. As my tank rolled across the river and began taking position, I was jolted by a sudden, crushing injury to my right leg. My knee bone was shattered. The pain was immediate and severe. But at that moment, there was no space for emotion. I didn't ask to be evacuated. I stayed down in the cold sand, in that exposed position, until the last tank of my regiment had crossed.

That decision wasn't about ego. It wasn't defiance. It came from years of living by one principle: *People First, Mission Always.*

When I stepped out of uniform and into a business suit, people expected me to recalibrate. Fit in. But that same fire came with me. I didn't try to blend in. I carried forward the same mission-first mindset I'd lived by for decades. A few were puzzled. They'd ask how I managed to stay so committed without knowing corporate jargon.

The truth? You don't need to decode passion. It speaks for itself.

That kind of passion speaks loudest when there's no audience. I remember lying in the cold sand that December, the pain in my knee sharp and unrelenting. I could feel, in that instant, that something was ending, something I had built my entire life around. But leaving wasn't an option. Not until the last tank had crossed. That operation and choice cost me my leg and my military future, but at that moment, the mission and my men came first. That willingness to stay, to keep moving forward on the mission when fear would've been easier, comes from something far deeper than duty. It's a passion that accepts the suffering, not for glory, but because the cause is worth it.

People often mistake enthusiasm for passion. One starts strong and fades fast. The other stays the course. Enthusiasm lights up the first step. Passion walks through fire to get to the last.

I've seen CEOs lose their footing under pressure. And I've seen soldiers with broken bones drag themselves forward because they were anchored to something bigger than their own comfort. That edge didn't come from training manuals. It came from belief.

Take away the title, the corner office, the applause. If someone's still leading, pushing, and still showing up with purpose, you know it's not the position that drives them. It's passion. The moment people around you realize you're more attached to your job title than to what you stand for, they stop following with trust and start following with silence. That's not leadership. That's mere existence.

When people ask me what keeps a leader from folding under pressure, it's never the bonuses or promotions. It's the reason they started. It's the clarity they carry in their gut when everything else is falling apart.

Before you keep reading, ask yourself one question.

Would you still do what you do if there were no applause waiting at the end?

If the answer is yes, that's where this conversation begins.

Cultivating Passion in Military Leadership

Passion in the military doesn't arrive as a motivational surge. It's instilled. Slowly. Deliberately. Day after day, without shortcuts or applause. The system doesn't teach passion. It builds it into your wiring.

When I joined the National Defence Academy, we weren't greeted with a welcome speech. We were broken down. Rebuilt. Put through drills that tested the mind more than the body. Every morning started with the same sharp clarity: show up, no matter what. That's where passion begins. In repetition. In discipline.

Discipline is often mistaken for control. It's not. It's clarity under pressure. It removes the fog. You know what needs to be done. You know why you're doing it. And you do it whether you feel like it or not. That process begins in training, but it doesn't stop there.

There's a reason cadets stand taller when they pass out of the academy. It's not the uniform. It's the clarity that seeps in. You learn quickly that the mission is always bigger than you. And once that's absorbed, your actions stop being conditional.

That clarity settles in over time, shaped by what's asked of you and what you learn to expect from yourself. For me, it came down to three things that were stamped into our thinking, not through lectures but through action: *Mission, Values, and Pride.* The mission reminded us why we were there in the first place. Values held us steady when decisions got harder. And pride came from knowing you carried something on your shoulders that others had carried before you, and you were expected to carry it forward without compromise. No one explained it. You just lived it. And once it took hold, it didn't leave.

In the Indian Army, we had a code that stayed with us long after parades and drills. The Chetwode Motto was carved into the walls of the Indian Military Academy, and more importantly, into us.

The safety, honor, and welfare of your country comes first, always and every time.

The honor, welfare and comfort of the men you command comes next.

Your own ease, comfort, and safety come last, always and every time.

Those three lines weren't quoted in passing. They were lived. Every decision, every order, every risk was weighed against that sequence. And it wasn't forced. It made sense. The moment the mission becomes clear, the rest aligns.

We didn't carry passion in our voices. We carried it in our readiness. On the way, we prepped for exercises, checked our weapons, and kept our uniforms sharp. Every small act fed into something larger. That's how the military works. It doesn't speak in slogans. It speaks through examples.

Camaraderie plays a bigger role than most realize. You train with your men, eat with them, and bleed with them. In operations, there are no spectators. When one man falters, another picks up the slack. Not out of instruction, but because failure isn't something you let a comrade carry alone. Soldiers, when asked what made them risk their lives for a comrade, always give the same answer, "because we knew they would have done exactly the same for us." That kind of trust isn't taught in a classroom. It's built day by day, through shared hardship and silent understanding.

There was a mission during my time with the Indian Peacekeeping Force in Sri Lanka that still sits with me. We were operating in an area controlled by a rebel group. They didn't follow any conventional rules. The environment was tense and unpredictable. For days, we stayed on high alert. Every movement had to be measured. Every decision mattered.

What I remember most clearly wasn't the threat. It was the way the team held together under that kind of pressure. Nobody waited to be told what needed to be done. Everyone knew the mission. Everyone knew their place in it. The discipline, the trust, the quiet readiness, it was all there. No drama, no shortcuts. Just a group of men who understood the weight of what they were carrying, and who refused to let each other down.

Passion shows itself in the smallest details. How a soldier polishes his boots before a field exercise. How a young officer refuses to let fatigue seep into his tone while giving orders. It's in the pride of wearing the regimental badge, the weight of which is heavier than the rank on the shoulder.

Traditions play their part too. The passing out parade isn't just a ceremony. It's the closing of one chapter and the beginning of something far more demanding. Traditions like these remind us that we belong to something older than ourselves. That history carries weight. And responsibility.

There is pride in wearing the same badge that others have worn into battle. Not because of the past alone, but because you are expected to carry it forward without compromise. That expectation doesn't create pressure. It builds resolve.

I've seen soldiers spring to their feet after being severely wounded, simply because their team was still under threat. I've seen men push through exhaustion, not for medals or promotion, but because the mission demanded it.

Passion in the military doesn't roar. It stays quiet. It stays focused. It doesn't need a stage. It needs clarity, repetition, and something worth standing for.

That is how it is cultivated. And once it takes root, it doesn't leave you.

Translating Passion to Corporate Leadership

When I stepped out of uniform, I wasn't stepping into a prepared role. I had no management degree, no background in business operations, and no exposure to market strategy. I had served twenty-five years in the Army, led men in battle, commanded a tank regiment, and participated in two United Nations missions in Cambodia. But now I was standing at the threshold of something entirely different. I had no job, no formal qualification for the corporate world, no house, and not enough money. What I did have was clarity, resilience, and a sense of duty that had been drilled into me since I was fifteen.

I joined NIIT without any prior business experience. The transition was not easy. I had to recalibrate my mindset, learn from scratch, and absorb everything I could from those around me, including my juniors. I was stepping into a room where no one owed me respect, and my military rank held no weight. What helped me stay grounded was the decision to focus on what I carried, not what I lacked, and the willingness to learn from anyone who knew more than I did. Titles didn't matter. If someone had knowledge that could help me grow, I listened. That attitude of openness, combined with leadership shaped under real pressure, and a mission-first mindset, helped me build forward with clarity.

NIIT had a mission I connected with immediately - Bringing people and Computers together successfully. That statement wasn't decorative. It was operational. It gave direction, and that direction gave me something I could anchor to. At the core, it was the same structure I had lived by in the Army. A mission that wasn't optional. A purpose that didn't shift with convenience.

As I stepped into various roles at NIIT and eventually into international business, spanning operations across forty countries, I stayed aligned with the one principle I knew well: purpose before the process. That clarity helped guide decisions through uncertainty and pressure.

There was a time during a particularly demanding phase of business restructuring when pressure came from every direction. Externally, markets were shifting. Internally, there was resistance. In those moments, it would have been easier to stall, to wait, or to act for optics. But the way I had been trained didn't allow for reaction under pressure. We had always been taught to plan fast, decide clearly, and execute with commitment. I applied the same mindset to those moments. We made the right calls and acted on them with speed and ownership. That period demanded focus, and focus came from staying connected to the mission.

In the Army, we don't do things for recognition. We do them because they are the right thing to do. I noticed in business that when people work for applause, their energy fades the moment recognition doesn't show up. That's when they burn out. Passion doesn't need noise. It shows itself through action, especially when no one is watching.

Another lesson that carried over was the role of the team. In the tank regiment I commanded, success didn't rest on one person. The gunner, the driver, and the commander each had a job to do in the tank, and each one relied on the other. The tank was not just a machine but a brotherhood in motion. If one slipped, the entire tank operations were affected. As well as the interdependence between a tank commander, troop leader, squadron commander, and the commanding officer. Every level of command has a cohesive role to play. Faltering at one level carries an adverse impact on the overall operations. I've seen the same thing happen in the corporate world. When leaders lose sight of their people and start managing dashboards instead of relationships, they end up tracking numbers, not building teams. You can count heads on payroll, but that won't tell you how many actually trust the one leading them. That's the difference between headcount and heart count. And the only way to earn that kind of trust is through action, not instruction.

That approach shaped how I led, whether it was on the field or across international business. People First, Mission Always wasn't written on a wall; it was carried into every decision, especially when the pressure rose. In the Army, I had seen firsthand that when your men know you'll stand with them, they'll stand for the mission. Later, in business, that same clarity helped build teams across cultures and time zones. It reminded me to never lose sight of the people behind the outcomes. When people know they matter, they bring their best to what needs to be done. That's how progress holds, and how trust turns into action.

Over the years, I didn't maintain energy by tracking progress on spreadsheets. I measured it through alignment. When your work is clear in your mind, when you know what you're building, then the weight of the task doesn't exhaust you. It sharpens you.

For anyone stepping into leadership, there's one question that makes all the difference: What are you really serving? If that answer is shallow, pressure will expose it. If that answer is solid, you'll stay anchored no matter how rough things get.

In the military, we're trained to stay ready without waiting for approval. In business, that same mindset becomes an edge. You act without waiting to feel ready. You lead without waiting for permission. And when passion is grounded in mission, it doesn't flare up and burn out. It holds steady. That kind of passion doesn't drain you. It propels you.

Reflection and Action

Leadership fueled by passion has the power to stay steady through pressure, change, and challenge. But even strong passion needs to be renewed sometimes. It needs space and focus. These three simple but important questions are here to help you check whether your fire is still clear and whether it's moving you in the direction you truly want to go.

1. GOT and NOT Inventory

This exercise helped me recalibrate when the ground beneath my feet changed. Take a sheet of paper and create two columns. On one side, write what you've GOT, such as your experience, your instincts, and your personal edge. On the other hand, write what you think you're missing, that is your NOTs. Now ask yourself: Which side do you lead from most often? If you're stuck in NOT, it's time to shift.

2. The Unfiltered Pulse Check

Ask yourself, with honesty: Why am I leading? Strip away the position, the perks, the recognition. Would you still show up with the same intent? Or has it quietly become about holding ground instead of moving forward?

3. Trace the Last Spark

Think back to the last time you felt fully engaged, not busy, not occupied, but involved. What were you working on? Who were you with? What made it matter? Go back there. Something in that moment holds a clue to what still drives you.

From Inner Fire to Steady Direction

Real passion doesn't need a microphone. It needs clarity. Purpose. A reason to endure when the energy dips and the noise fades. That kind of passion builds resolve.

The next step in this journey is not about turning up the heat. It is about channeling that fire into something steady, a mission you can follow, values you can live by, and a sense of pride that anchors you when the ground shifts. These three elements, which I would like to call the MVP, became the pillars that gave meaning to every decision, every risk, and every commitment I carried, first in uniform and later, across global boardrooms.

That structure is where passion turns into leadership. Let's go there.

<u>Key Takeaways</u>

- **Passion is the fuel of leadership:** Passion comes from the heart. It is the willingness to give your all, even suffer if needed, for what you deeply believe in. It is the force that fuels meaningful leadership.

- **Mission answers the question: "Why do I exist?"** When your mission is clear, it anchors every action. Like a tank's gun locked on target, your mission keeps you steady through turbulence and change.

- **Values guide us when the ground shakes:** Your values are what you turn to when plans collapse. They shape decisions under stress and reflect who you are, not just what you say.

- **Pride is not ego; it's identity with honor:** Pride means holding your head high because of what you represent. When grounded in honor, it drives excellence and resilience.

- **MVP: Mission, Values, and Pride are the foundation of Passion:** These three tenets, etched into the spirit of a soldier, can equally guide leaders in business and life to lead with courage and clarity.

- **Without Passion, leadership becomes transactional:** When passion is absent, leadership turns into management. When present, it inspires belief, ownership, and transformation.

- **A strong WHY fuels a resilient HOW:** Challenges become stepping stones when your mission is deeply personal. Your 'why' must be so strong that quitting is not an option.

- **Passion is contagious:** When a leader lives their mission, upholds their values, and carries pride in who they are, it creates a ripple effect of energy and commitment.

Chapter

02

MVP – The Framework of Passion

"If your Mission is inspiring and clear, your Values are infused in your being, and your Pride is ingrained in everything you do, you will be invincible."

That statement has stayed with me for years because I've seen it hold true in situations where motivation alone would never have been enough. Passion can carry you through the first stretch, but it cannot hold the weight of responsibility on its own. The leaders who endure, who inspire trust when pressure mounts, are the ones who build their passion on something deeper and more structured.

In the military, we didn't talk about frameworks in theory. We lived them in action. Early on, we were taught that clarity leads to action. You must know where you're headed before you're asked to lead anyone else. That's where it all began. With a mission that wasn't optional. With values that didn't shift when things got hard. And with a sense of pride that made you show up even when no one was watching.

As I look back, the moments where I felt most grounded, whether in uniform or in the corporate space, were never fueled by emotion alone. They were backed by a quiet alignment between what I was doing, why

I was doing it, and who I believed myself to be while doing it. That's the space where passion strengthens. It becomes part of your operating system, not a reaction to circumstance.

The transition from a structured military environment into a more flexible world of business exposed something interesting. Many professionals carry talent, knowledge, and ambition. But without a clear sense of direction or personal alignment, I saw their energy scatter under pressure. That's when I knew the structure I had carried from the Army had something to offer in this world, too. It wasn't a model drawn on whiteboards. It was built in the field, in decision-making moments where lives and missions were at stake.

That structure can be summed up in three anchors: Mission, Values, and Pride, what I call the MVP framework.

This framework is personal. I have lived it across two very different phases of my life. In the years ahead, as I stepped into leadership roles across global markets, I kept falling back on these three facets. Whether I was dealing with business setbacks or coaching senior leaders, the pattern stayed the same. When these three were in place, people didn't need pep talks. They found their own clarity.

Passion has a better chance of staying alive when it rests on something stable. You begin to notice this when decisions get harder, when timelines shrink, and when people start looking to you for steadiness instead of excitement. In those moments, it's not charm or pressure-handling techniques that help. What helps is knowing where you're anchored.

I've come to rely on three points of reference. Mission gives me purpose. Values keep me steady. Pride reminds me why the work matters. When those three line up, you stop drifting. You begin to lead with intent that doesn't shake when the conditions do.

The deeper I went into leadership, whether on the field, in the boardroom, or while coaching others, the more clearly I saw these three at play. Each one carried its own weight. Together, they created the kind of alignment that made the work worth showing up for, day after day.

Let's start with where it begins for most people who lead with intent. Mission. The one thing that sharpens your focus before the decision is even made.

Mission – The Guiding Star

Passion doesn't hold its shape unless it's anchored. One of those anchors, for me, has always been the mission.

Once you know why you exist in a role, the weight of the work becomes something you carry with intent, not effort. You're no longer trying to stay motivated. You're committed to the outcome because it defines your presence there. That shift happens the moment the mission becomes clear.

In the Army, we were trained to lead with this kind of clarity from the very start. There was no ambiguity. You were expected to know your mission and act like it mattered. Every step in training was designed to shape that mindset, physically, mentally, and emotionally. We were pushed beyond our comfort zones so that, under pressure, the mission stayed intact even when everything else felt unstable.

Most people who've spent time in the military will tell you the same thing: we didn't wake up driven by excitement. We were driven by focus. That focus came from the mission.

And the clarity wasn't limited to drills or commands. It was carved into how we were expected to think. You don't need anything more than that to know where your priorities stand.

Even in tank warfare, the analogy carries. In a live operation, once a gun is stabilized and locked onto a target, the tank may shift direction or maneuver based on terrain and conditions, but the gun remains laser locked on the target. That's how we were trained to treat the mission. Adapt where needed, but never lose focus.

You might remember the riverbed incident I mentioned earlier. My leg was shattered during that operation. The decision to delay evacuation wasn't about heroism. It was about finishing what we started, ensuring the tanks crossed, and the mission was completed. That lens, that the mission matters more than the moment, stayed with me long after I left the military. The tanks hadn't crossed yet. The mission wasn't done. Quitting was not an option. That lens doesn't leave you once it's in place. It holds steady whether you're in combat or in a boardroom.

One of the crystal clear examples of being "laser-locked" on the mission, even in the face of certain death, is the story of Second Lieutenant Arun Khetarpal, Param Vir Chakra (Posthumous), of The 17 Poona Horse during the Battle of Basantar in 1971. At just 21 years old, Khetarpal embodied what it means to live and die for the mission. In the thick of battle, despite his tank taking a direct hit and catching fire, he refused to abandon it. When ordered to pull back, his words over the radio were unwavering: "No, Sir. I will not abandon my tank. My gun is still working, and I will get these bastards." He went on to destroy multiple enemy tanks until he was fatally wounded. Khetarpal didn't just know his mission, he became it. That kind of commitment doesn't come from motivation; it comes from an internal compass set so firmly on purpose that not even death can turn it off. That is the kind of spirit the MVP framework calls us to build, a mission so embedded in your identity that retreat is never an option.

At NIIT, I saw what a clear and deeply embedded mission could create. From the very beginning in 1981, the organization was anchored by a single-line commitment: *Bringing People and Computers Together, Successfully.* It wasn't a slogan. It was a north star. That one sentence carried the weight of everything that followed: decisions, strategies, partnerships, and culture. It didn't need elaborate branding because it offered something stronger: *clarity.* And clarity, when it's real, doesn't stay at the top; it travels. It reaches the front line. It shapes how people respond to setbacks, how they make decisions under pressure, and why they stay committed when results take time.

By the time NIIT had trained over 35 million people across 40 countries, the original mission had not been diluted. That's the strength of a guiding line that isn't revisited every quarter, it's lived every day. I experienced firsthand how a mission like that doesn't just define what a company does; it defines how people show up to it.

In many other corporate environments, a different pattern often emerged. Many organizations had goals. Teams had plans. But the anchor, a clearly articulated and lived mission, was often missing. You could feel the drift when pressure built up. Meetings would lose direction, decisions lacked depth, and energy would scatter across too many tasks with no shared thread holding it all together.

That's when I realized something: without a mission that is both understood and believed in, alignment becomes fragile. Strategy becomes reactive. And when setbacks arrive, as they always do, people look for direction, but find only tasks.

Whether you're building a company, leading a team, or figuring out your own direction, your mission sits at the center. It doesn't need to sound impressive. It needs to be sharp. It should be something you can repeat without second-guessing and hold onto when things get messy.

I often ask leaders one question: Can you say why you're doing what you're doing without reaching for a title or a pitch? If that sentence isn't clear in your own mind, it won't carry weight with anyone else? The mission begins at the core, not with *what* you do or *how* you do it, but *why* you do it.

That's the difference between movement and momentum. Simon Sinek calls it starting with the "Why", the inner circle that drives everything outward. When leaders begin with *Why*, decisions carry meaning. Communication becomes authentic. People don't just comply, they connect.

And once your "Why" is clear, don't polish it. Live it. Let it show in how you lead. Let it guide your tone in a tense meeting, your choices in a crowded day, and your resilience when things don't go to plan. A real mission doesn't need repetition to be remembered, it shows up in how you show up.

If you're trying to define that for yourself or your organization, start here:

- Who is served when your work is done well?

- What result is worth holding the line for, even when nothing is easy?

- What must remain true, even when the strategy has to shift?

That's where your mission sits. Once you find it, the rest starts to fall into place. Goals make sense. Plans tighten. And your presence, as a leader, gains weight without needing explanation.

Values – The Moral Compass

If your mission tells you where you're going, your values decide how you'll get there.

I've seen brilliant strategies fall apart because the values behind them were weak. I've also seen teams stand their ground in chaos, not because they were the best trained, but because they knew what they stood for. That's what values do. They step in when conditions break down and clarity thins out.

In the Army, values weren't written to impress. They were meant to hold up under pressure. The values were clear: integrity, loyalty, duty, respect, honor, courage, and selfless service. But those words weren't for display. They were tested in decisions where comfort wasn't an option, and were infused with action, blood, sweat, and spirit.

Leading soldiers into a combat zone isn't about inspiring them with speeches. No one's listening for words when bullets are flying. What matters is what they've seen in you before that moment. Whether you meant what you said. Whether you stood your ground when it wasn't convenient. That's what earns trust. That's what builds belief.

I remember a question someone once asked a group of soldiers: "Why would you risk your life for the man next to you?" And the answer came without hesitation, "Because he'd do the same for me." That's not sentiment. That's shared values in action. That kind of bond doesn't form through instructions. It builds when values are repeated in small, unseen moments until they become instinct.

There's a story from the aftermath of the Hiroshima bombing that I've never forgotten. A young Japanese boy was seen carrying the body of his little brother on his back. A soldier nearby noticed him and gently suggested that he set the body down to rest since it might be heavy for him. The body answered softly, "He's not heavy. He's my brother." He kept walking with steady steps, focused on giving his brother a proper farewell. What moved him was a deep sense of care and responsibility that lived within him. He didn't need to say anything more; his actions were clear. This is the kind of strength that values bring. They hold steady in moments when the world feels heavy. They shape how we respond when there is no one to guide us. And they remind us that leadership, at its core, begins with how we carry what matters the most.

In the corporate world, I began to notice that the strongest values were often reflected in quiet decisions made under pressure rather than in what was written on a wall or said in meetings. At NIIT, one of the first lines I came across in the Vision statement read: "We, NIIT, believe that our growth is the derivative of the growth of each one of us." That wasn't a throwaway line. I saw it play out in real decisions, especially when it came to people. It showed up in how hiring was done, how colleagues were treated, and how difficult choices were made in uncertain times. When values are real, they don't get shelved during a crisis, they get louder.

One of the most powerful corporate examples of values in action comes from the early 1980s, when Johnson & Johnson faced a crisis that could have broken the company. Seven people died after taking Tylenol capsules laced with cyanide. There was panic, public outrage, and uncertainty everywhere. The business implications were massive. But the leadership at J&J didn't flinch. They pulled over 31 million bottles off the shelves across the U.S., issued public warnings, and stopped production immediately because their Credo put customers first. That credo didn't gather dust in a drawer. It guided every decision in that moment.

Even when there was no clear evidence that J&J was at fault, they acted as if the responsibility was theirs. They redesigned packaging to introduce tamper-proof seals and regained public trust not through PR campaigns, but through action rooted in values. Their response is still studied in business schools, because it showed what happens when a company truly lives by its principles.

Whether in uniform or in a boardroom, values aren't real until they're tested. It's what you do in the hard moments that tells the truth about what you stand for. Values influence how leaders act when no one is watching. They shape how you treat the people who can't offer you anything in return. They set the tone in crisis, and they often determine whether trust survives a bad quarter.

But here's the truth: values can't be borrowed. They have to be your own. You can't copy what sounds right. You have to ask yourself what actually holds weight for you.

So ask yourself now: What do I stand by when comfort, convenience, and personal gain are removed from the equation? What do I protect even when the pressure's on? What do I refuse to compromise, regardless of who's asking?

If the answers don't come easily, don't rush them. Spend time with those questions. Your values aren't meant to sound good. They're meant to stand up when everything else starts shaking.

Once you've found them, don't try to showcase them. Let them show how you respond when you don't have time to think. That's where the real measure of a leader sits.

Pride – The Fuel of Commitment and Excellence

Pride, when rooted in something meaningful, becomes fuel. It keeps people steady through grind, loss, fatigue, and long stretches where nothing comes easy. I've seen it hold men together in combat. I've seen it lift teams through corporate uncertainty. But it has to be real. It has to be earned. Otherwise, it turns into ego. And the ego doesn't carry weight. It collapses under pressure.

In the Army, pride isn't an abstract idea. It's visible. It's felt. It's lived. You see it in the way a soldier wears his regimental badge, not just like an emblem but like a commitment. That badge isn't a decoration. It carries a history. It tells you where you come from and what you're expected to carry forward. I've seen soldiers rally around that symbol without needing to be told why. Because it's not the object, it's what it stands for.

I still remember the first time I wore the badge of The Scinde Horse and later of 46 Armoured Regiment. That wasn't just a badge or an emblem. That was a responsibility. When you put it on, you don't represent yourself anymore. You represent every soldier who wore it before you, and everyone who will come after. That kind of pride doesn't make you arrogant. It keeps you accountable.

In the military, pride in the Regimental badge, pride in the battle honors and glorious traditions of the Regiment, and pride in the Mission, is a key battle-winning and defining factor.

We wear the badge on our headgear, which is a unifying symbol of pride, respect, and honor. These are symbols and emblems of inspiration and intense Pride in the Regiment, to the extent that soldiers rally around and are willing to lay down their lives for the accomplishment of the Mission and protection of the pride, glory, and reputation of the Regiment.

It's easy to confuse pride with stubbornness. That's not what I'm talking about here. I'm talking about the kind of pride that makes you hold the standard even when nobody's watching. The kind that keeps you from cutting corners because the job carries your name, and your name still means something to you.

At NIIT, pride had a quiet strength. It could be sensed in the way people carried themselves and spoke about their work. There was a deep sense of belonging that came through in conversations and in how teams stayed committed, even during tough phases. I've seen colleagues uphold the company's name with the same care they would give to their own. This kind of culture grows when people believe in what they're building together. When identity and purpose align, performance follows naturally. It finds its own rhythm and builds a strength that does not fade easily.

That kind of culture can't be built through handbooks or slogans. It grows when people begin to see themselves in the work they do. At NIIT, that connection was real. It shaped how decisions were made, how teams responded to uncertainty, and how individuals carried themselves even when no one was watching.

In other corporate environments I've come across, the picture wasn't always the same. This isn't to generalize, but in many places, I've seen what can happen when pride is missing. People do what's asked, no more, no less. They wait for instructions, shift blame when things go wrong, and disengage when appreciation is absent. It's not a lack of competence. It's a quiet erosion of belief. The belief that their contribution matters.

In both the Army and business, I've seen that morale rarely breaks because of skill. It breaks when people stop seeing the value in what they bring. Pride restores that. It anchors people. It tells them that what they do carries weight, even when no one says it out loud.

I've often asked the leaders I coach how proud they are of what they stand for. Can they confidently say that their name adds weight to the work they do? Do the people they lead feel that same weight in themselves?

Self-esteem and self-image are not soft traits. They directly shape output. I've never seen anyone outperform their view of themselves for long. So if pride isn't present, performance won't hold. Culture will leak. And people will slowly disconnect from the very thing they once cared about.

This isn't about walking around with inflated confidence. It's about standing inside your role with a steady spine. It's about honoring your part in something larger, whether that's a team, a regiment, or an organization.

When pride is clean and connected to service, it doesn't need noise. It shows up in consistency. It sharpens commitment. And it builds a kind of quiet momentum that doesn't fizzle out when conditions shift.

That's the kind of pride that wins battles. And more importantly, keeps people worth following.

Applying MVP to Leadership

I've been asked more than once how I stayed steady during unpredictable stretches of my career. The answer has never changed. I've always returned to the same three anchors: Mission, Values, and Pride.

This wasn't a model I picked up from a course. It was built in the field, under pressure. First in uniform. Then later, in boardrooms where the stakes were different, but the need for clarity was exactly the same.

Mission, Values, and Pride aren't slogans. They're stabilizers. When applied well, they bring a kind of internal alignment that doesn't shake when circumstances shift.

In the military, every action was filtered through those three lenses. Why does this matter? Is it being done in line with what we believe? And can I put my name behind it with pride? That framework kept teams steady in the face of stress. It helped leaders take tough calls without flinching. It gave people the courage to follow orders when there was no time for long explanations.

In business, I've watched MVP work in quieter but equally powerful ways. During a major restructuring phase at NIIT, we found ourselves dealing with intense market shifts. There were moments when pressure was high across departments. What kept the team steady wasn't optimism. It was clarity. Everyone understood the mission. People trusted that the decisions being made were in line with the organization's values. And there was a deep sense of pride in staying the course with integrity. That was enough to keep us from falling apart under pressure. That was MVP in action.

I've also seen this framework resonate with entrepreneurs I've coached. These are people working without the security of a title or a large system behind them. When their mission was clear, their pace held strong. When their values were personal, their decisions stayed clean. And when they were proud of what they were building, they found the resilience to push forward when momentum dipped.

Most people miss this: Motivation fades, and circumstances shift. But if you're grounded in a mission that matters, if you act from values that matter, and if you take pride in what you are inspired to do, resilience stops being something you need to summon. It becomes your natural state.

So, how do you bring MVP into your own leadership? Start simple.

First, write your mission in one sentence. Don't dress it up. Don't try to impress. Just ask yourself why your work exists and who it serves.

Next, identify three values you refuse to compromise. Not the ones that sound good. The ones that shape how you actually act. Think back to the toughest decision you've made recently. What guided you? That's where your values live.

Finally, ask yourself. What are you proud of today? And if the answer feels weak, find out where you disconnected. Was it the mission? Were your values wanting? Did you show up in a way that didn't feel like you?

This isn't a checklist. It's a system for self-alignment. When MVP sits at the center of your leadership, clarity becomes automatic. Your energy stays focused. You know why you're doing what you're doing. And you stop relying on external validation to stay the course.

That's the real strength of MVP. It doesn't make leadership easier. It makes it clearer.

Reflection and Action

You don't build alignment by reading principles. You build it by checking your posture when no one's watching. This section isn't designed for ticking boxes. It's a chance to see what still holds, what's slipped, and where the recalibration needs to start.

1. The 60-Second Walkthrough

Close your eyes and walk through your last week like a fly on the wall. Don't look for achievements. Watch how you showed up.

- Did your actions match what you say you stand for?

- Were you rushed, reactive, scattered, or steady, intentional, engaged?

- Now open your eyes. What would someone else say you lead with, clarity or convenience?

2. The Five-Line Rulebook

Forget taglines and team charters. Write your own rulebook, five lines only. These are your personal non-negotiables, the principles you won't trade no matter the pressure.

Now check them against how you've handled conflict, feedback, or silence lately.

What line needs to be stronger? What line feels hollow? Adjust it until it reads like something you'd carry in your pocket, not to quote, but to live by.

3. The 3–3–3 Check

- Name three decisions this month you're proud of. Not for the outcome, but for how you chose.

- Name three moments where you flinched, hesitated, or blurred your own line.

- Name three actions you'll take next week that reinforce who you are and not what you do.

Write them down. Don't save them for later. Self-correction isn't weakness, it's how real leadership stays alive.

Alignment That Lasts

Clarity doesn't have to wait for a crisis. You don't need a breakdown to ask better questions or to realign with what matters. Crisis doesn't build character, it reveals it. And what it often reveals is whether your foundation was real to begin with.

That's where MVP becomes more than a framework. It becomes an anchor. When mission becomes your reason, values your guardrails, and pride your fuel, you stop chasing motivation. You lead from a place that doesn't shake every time conditions change.

The work ahead will pull you in many directions. There will be noise, distraction, and pressure to perform. What holds you steady isn't energy. It's alignment.

And that alignment is tested most when people enter the picture. That's where we go next. Because leadership is not a solo pursuit. It becomes real when others begin to align. And how they align depends on what you're really standing for when no one's clapping and the outcomes aren't guaranteed.

<u>Key Takeaways</u>

- **Mission brings clarity when noise sets in**: Your mission isn't a slogan, it's the reason you stay steady when conditions spiral. It sharpens focus and makes tough choices clearer.

- **Without a mission, momentum drifts:** Tasks lose meaning when purpose is missing. A clear "why" turns movement into direction and effort into intent.

- **Values are how you stay anchored under pressure:** When rules blur and situations test you, values guide the response. They hold steady where strategy cannot.

- **Real values show in quiet choices:** It's not about what's written on walls, it's about what you do when there's nothing to gain and no one to impress.

- **Pride adds weight to how you show up:** When you're proud of what you stand for, you carry your role like it matters, because it does.

- **True pride never shouts, it shows:** You see it in how corners aren't cut, how reputations are guarded, and how people hold themselves when no one is watching.

- **MVP is a muscle memory:** Built through repetition and real moments, this trio, Mission, Values, Pride, becomes the instinct that steadies leadership under fire.

- **Leadership rooted in MVP doesn't need constant motivation:** When your work aligns with your why, how, and who, you stop chasing energy. You start moving from alignment and inspiration.

People – The Heart of Leadership

What defines a great leader? Their strategy, or how their people feel under their leadership?

The effectiveness of a leader is not measured by strategies crafted in a boardroom or the brilliance of a five-year plan, but by the strength of relationships built, the trust nurtured, and the morale sustained during times of ambiguity, setbacks, and transition. Strategy may provide direction, but it is people who execute missions, rise in adversity, and ultimately shape the soul of any organization. A leader's ability to connect with people, invest in them, and ignite belief is what moves teams from compliance to commitment.

That understanding came while commanding a regiment that had to be battle-ready on short notice. It came in Sri Lanka, navigating the political tightrope between military action and civilian protection. It came in Cambodia, where officers from 33 nations had to trust each other in order to enforce peace. And it came while standing on corporate floors across the globe, listening more than speaking, learning as much from the frontline sales team in Delhi as from a strategy meeting in South Africa.

What became evident across those environments, whether in tanks or boardrooms, was that the defining attribute of every high-performing unit, military or corporate, was morale. And morale was not built by motivational speeches or compensation structures alone. It was built with care.

Caring is what turns leadership from something positional into something personal. It is what makes people not just follow instructions, but commit from the heart. Caring is dealing with people with empathy, compassion, and kindness. It's creating an atmosphere of safety, protection, belonging, and value. It's when people feel seen not as headcount but as heart count.

You don't need to pamper people to care for them. Caring isn't soft. It's disciplined. It's a tough decision to put people first, even when performance targets demand otherwise. It's guiding without diminishing. Correcting without humiliating. And believing in someone before they believe in themselves.

Caring also means stroking ambition, both visible and latent. It is the mark of a developmental leader to create opportunities for growth, exposure, and expertise. It's noticing potential before it's polished. Helping someone stretch into roles they didn't yet know they were ready for. Because when people feel cared for, they become courageous.

But even the best leaders have to guard against something subtle: allowing past disappointments to cloud present perception. One bad people experience can blur your lens. If you're not careful, you begin to see the next person through the shadows of the last. Great leaders know when to wipe their lenses clean. To meet people where they are, not where someone else left them.

In the Indian Army, the credo was clear. "The safety, honor, and welfare of your country comes first, always and every time. The honor, welfare, and comfort of the men you command comes next. Your own ease, comfort, and safety comes last, always and every time." These lines carried far beyond the commissioning day. It became the daily lens through which decisions were made. That same principle translated to every leadership seat occupied in the years that followed. Whether dealing with an underperforming business unit, a disengaged team, or a struggling colleague, the answer never started with policy. It started with presence.

There were moments when decisions had to be made that put people first, even when it appeared contrary to performance targets. There were times when holding space for someone's struggle or standing up for a junior executive's honest mistake meant risking backlash. But over time, those actions created cultures where people knew their leader had their backs. And when people feel that kind of psychological safety, they don't wait for instructions. They take initiative. They own the mission.

It is easy to lead when everything is going well. It is in the fog of uncertainty when plans unravel and pressure mounts that the quality of leadership is revealed. In those moments, it is not strategy documents that teams turn to. They look at the leader. They look for stability in their eyes, belief in their tone, and fairness in their decisions. They look to be led by someone who, regardless of their rank or role, lives by the motto: People First, Mission Always.

That phrase is not a theory. It has been lived through moments of crisis and clarity. Through injury and transition. Through foreign assignments and unfamiliar boardrooms. And through every phase, one truth has remained constant: when people know they matter, they give more than what is expected. They stay longer than required. They carry the mission as their own.

True leadership is measured in trust deposits. In the loyalty that shows up not because it is obligated, but because it is earned. In the resilience of a team that pushes forward not out of fear of failure, but from a shared belief that they are in it together.

And that begins when leaders choose to lead not from behind a desk, but from among the people.

Maintenance of Morale: The Invisible Force Behind Performance

In the military, there is a term that holds as much weight as any battlefield strategy: Maintenance of Morale. It is considered one of the essential principles of war. Not because it sounds good in leadership manuals, but because history has shown that no matter how advanced the equipment or how precise the plan, missions succeed or fail on the will of the people executing them.

Morale is what fuels the will to fight. It is the force that keeps soldiers moving when fatigue has numbed the body, when danger feels imminent, and when the outcome remains uncertain. It is that invisible current that runs through a Regiment and makes them push, not because they are told to, but because they want to.

Morale is often misunderstood in leadership conversations. It is seen as something soft. Peripheral. Nice to have. But in reality, it is a decisive factor in performance. And in the military, it is never left to chance. Morale is not pampering. It is built with clarity, training, and discipline.

When people are clear about the mission, equipped to succeed, and led with consistency and courage, morale is naturally sustained. When confusion sets in, or when leadership becomes reactive instead of intentional, morale begins to erode, quietly at first, then rapidly.

As a commander, I learned that morale wasn't something you infused on the day of battle. It was something you cultivated every day in between. It was in the tone you used during daily briefings. In how you trained your team to trust each other. In the discipline, you upheld, not to control, but to create confidence. And perhaps most importantly, in how you carried yourself when things got hard.

Morale, in its truest sense, is the emotional readiness of a team. It determines how much ownership they take. How far they'll go when the plan unravels. Whether they pause in fear or step forward in faith. And it doesn't live in motivational speeches. It lives in leadership presence.

Translating this into the corporate world, I saw the same truth apply. When teams knew why their work mattered, when they felt supported, not micromanaged, when they sensed that their leaders genuinely had their backs, morale grew stronger than deadlines. It translated into initiative. Into creative problem-solving. Into resilience.

I've walked into organizations where every incentive plan was in place, but morale was low. People were skilled, but stagnant. They had knowledge, but no spark. And I've walked into teams with tight resources but high morale, where people stayed late, supported each other, and delivered results that far exceeded expectations. The difference? Not perks. Not processed. Leadership that paid attention to morale.

And here's what I've seen firsthand: high morale fosters offensive spirit, grit, and the will to win. It creates an internal culture where people show up with infectious enthusiasm, not as a mood, but as a mindset. Where setbacks don't cause disengagement, but rather trigger resolve.

As leaders, we must ask ourselves often: What is the emotional state of my team right now? Are they engaged, or merely enduring? Am I creating clarity or confusion? Am I feeding morale through belief and consistency, or quietly draining it through neglect?

The greatest leaders I've worked with, whether on the battlefield or in business, understood this: people don't follow instructions in difficult times; they follow belief.

And belief is born when morale is maintained, not as an afterthought, but as a priority.

The Battle Within – Leading Yourself First

One of the most pivotal battles I have ever faced wasn't against an enemy across the border. It was against the voices within my own head.

I was commanding my tank regiment near the border on 11th December 1997, a day forever etched in my memory. We were mid-way through a river-crossing operation when an accident on my tank left me with a crushed knee and a decision that would change the direction of my life.

As I lay on the cold, wet bed of the Ravi River, refusing evacuation until every tank in my regiment completed the mission, I knew something had shifted. It wasn't just my leg that was broken, it was the sudden severing of my identity. Twenty-five years in uniform washed away in a matter of moments.

My military journey had been one of honor, responsibility, and steady progression. From the Indian Peace Keeping Force in Sri Lanka to peacekeeping missions in Cambodia and commanding my own regiment, I had been groomed for higher ranks and deeper responsibilities. Until that moment. Until the farewell to arms became real, and I was left facing not the battlefield, but myself.

I had no job in hand. No business qualification. Two sons were still finding their paths. A wife to support. And a haunting sense of having no idea who I was anymore. The voices started quietly, but they grew stronger. "You're not good enough for the corporate world." "You don't know how this world works." "You've come too far in one life to begin another." "You're too old to start again."

It was a dark season. And I had two choices: become a soldier to those voices or take command of my own mind.

That decision changed everything. I realized that the greatest battle is not on the field. It's in the mind. That 16 inches between the heart and the head can define everything. And if you lose there, it's only a matter of time before you lose outside as well. In those moments, I reminded myself of one principle that has never failed me: *your mind is a battlefield; be its commander, not its soldier.*

If you are a soldier of your mind, you follow its fears, its conditioning, and its tendency to seek safety in the familiar. But if you become its commander, you take charge of what you allow, what you reject, and what you install. And that makes all the difference.

Here are the seven steps that helped me become the commander of my mind and not its soldier. I coined the acronym MASIBAF.

Step 1 – Monitor

I began by observing. Not reacting, just watching the mental chatter. I took note of what I was telling myself each time uncertainty knocked on the door. I started a self-talk diary. Even today, I tell leaders this: your most powerful conversations are the ones you have with yourself. Monitor them. They shape your identity far more than you realize.

Step 2 – Arrest

Next, I became intentional about identifying thoughts that were holding me back. Thoughts of inferiority. Of insecurity. For comparison. I captured them as if I were isolating a threat in the field. If left unchecked, they would take root, grow, and shape decisions from a place of fear. Capturing meant calling them out, not letting them fester in silence.

Step 3 – Speak Out

This step was a game-changer. I began to speak to those thoughts directly. Six words became my mental reset button: "Thank you – but – no thank you."

Why "thank you"? Because those voices, those old conditionings, were doing their job: trying to protect me. But I didn't need protection. I needed perspective. So I acknowledged them, then dismissed them.

Thank you for trying to keep me safe. But no, thank you, I have a mission to fulfill.

Step 4 – Install

Once I created space by removing disempowering thoughts, I filled that space with empowering ones. I reminded myself of the assets I still carried:

- I had led people in crisis.

- I have operated in volatile environments.

- I understood strategy, pressure, and performance under fire.

- I knew how to lead people, not just through hierarchy, but through trust.

I installed new beliefs. I have value. I have transferable strength. I will learn what I don't know. I am more than enough.

I visualized what I wanted. Not vaguely, but vividly. I pictured myself leading businesses, impacting lives globally, and building something that mattered. I saw it before I saw it. And I gave myself permission to believe it.

Step 5 – Believe

It's one thing to visualize success. It's another thing to believe you belong in it. I reminded myself that belief is not a soft sentiment, it is fuel. I began feeding belief more than I fed doubt. I developed what I call a burning desire, a concept born in military history, where options were removed and commitment was non-negotiable.

Retreat becomes easy when it's available. But belief thrives when you remove the exit door and stand firm in your intention. I chose belief over backup plans. And it showed.

Step 6 – Act

With belief in place, I stepped forward. At times afraid. Often unsure. But I acted. I didn't wait for mastery to make a move. I understood this from my military days: you don't wait for certainty, you lead into it.

In rooms where I was the least experienced, I contributed. In meetings where I could have stayed silent, I asked questions. And each action made the next easier. Every step into the unfamiliar made the fear fade. Action has a way of shrinking what imagination amplifies.

Step 7 – Feel Good Now

This step was about emotional alignment. I practiced what it felt like to already be in motion toward my vision. I lived from that emotional state, even before the outcomes showed up. It wasn't fake confidence, it was borrowed faith from the future I was building.

That feeling kept me grounded. It kept me focused on building, not fearing. When belief becomes emotional, it gains traction. And when your emotions are aligned with your mission, your leadership becomes magnetic.

These seven steps (MASIBAF) didn't just help me through one season. They became the foundation of my self-leadership across the next 15 years in corporate life, where I grew from regional leadership to heading international business across 40 countries.

They helped me stay anchored in moments of self-doubt, navigate transitions, and show up with clarity and strength for those I was leading.

Because if there's one thing I've learned, it is this: leadership begins long before you stand in front of a team. It begins when you stand in front of the mirror and decide who will lead you. Your fears? Or your faith and values?

And before I lead others with People First, Mission Always, I must first lead myself, with clarity, courage, and the discipline to command my own mind.

Building and Maintaining Trust

When I reflect on the most effective teams I've led, whether in a tank formation navigating hostile terrain or in a corporate boardroom negotiating international deals, one thing stands out above all: trust was never optional. It was the operating system. Without it, we were just a group of people working side by side. With it, we became a team moving with clarity, speed, and commitment.

Trust doesn't begin with systems or policies. It begins with people, how they show up, how consistent they are, and whether their words align with their actions. I've come to believe that trust is simply confidence. Confidence is born out of two non-negotiables: character and competence. Not one or the other, but both. One without the other creates an imbalance. A character without competence may win hearts but not outcomes. Competence without character might hit short-term targets but will never build enduring teams.

In the Army, trust wasn't a workshop topic. It was a matter of life. There's a moment I've shared before, of a young soldier who, without hesitation, risked his life to pull a wounded comrade to safety. When I asked him why, his response was quiet and without drama: "Because he would have done it for me." That sentence has stayed with me for years, not for its poetic value, but for its raw, unfiltered truth. It reminded me that trust at its purest isn't about directives. It's about belief. A belief that the person beside you will show up, stand up, and not walk away when it matters most.

That same standard carried over as I transitioned into the corporate world. When I stepped into NIIT after laying down my uniform, I wasn't carrying my rank, I was carrying my principles. I had to build trust again, brick by brick, in an environment where no one owed me loyalty. My past didn't guarantee anything. And so, I started the same way I had in every new command: by listening first, showing up consistently, and doing exactly what I said I would.

One of the most powerful ways to build trust in any environment is radical transparency. Speak the truth, especially when it's uncomfortable.

In the corporate space, this meant being open about both wins and losses, setting clear expectations, and not sugarcoating challenges. It also meant being accessible, removing layers of hierarchy, and allowing people to speak freely, without fear of repercussion.

The mindset that helped anchor this was always the same: People First, Mission Always. When a team knows that they are valued beyond their output and that they will not be sacrificed at the altar of optics, they begin to operate differently. They stop holding back. They start thinking bigger. And they take ownership beyond their roles.

Trust is not a one-time decision. It is a daily investment. It's how you respond when someone falters. It's whether you protect your people in public and hold honest conversations in private. It's whether your presence brings comfort or caution. And it is built far more on how you carry the ordinary than how you handle the exceptional.

During one of our major skill development and expansion projects in South Africa, I saw firsthand how critical trust becomes when working across cultures and time zones. The success of that initiative didn't rest on spreadsheets. It came down to relationships, how we listened to local leaders, included them in decision-making, and treated them as partners, not placeholders. Trust was our strategy, and it worked.

Trust can't be borrowed. It must be earned. And once broken, it takes twice the effort to rebuild if at all.

It is not what people say about you in meetings that matters most. It's the conversations they have when you're not in the room. That's where real trust or the lack of it is revealed.

So, I ask myself, and every leader I work with: Would your team place your name in the "trusted" column without hesitation? Have you earned it?

Because when trust is present, performance follows. People don't need to be managed. They need to be believed in.

And when they feel that belief, they will move mountains not because they have to, but because they want to.

Developing Empathy and Emotional Intelligence

Over the years, I've come to realize that the mark of a leader isn't just how they respond to pressure; it's how they relate to people when no one is watching. It's in the moments between tasks, in the pauses between meetings, in how attentively they listen, and in whether people feel safe bringing their full selves to the conversation.

Empathy is not a weakness. It is wisdom with awareness. It is the ability to sense what's going on beneath the surface without needing it to be explained. When people feel seen, not for their output but for their experience, they begin to operate from trust rather than transaction. They become more open, more engaged, and more committed, not because they have to, but because they want to.

Emotional intelligence, in my experience, begins with self-awareness. The ability to recognize what state I am in, how it is shaping my tone, and whether I am leading from calm or from chaos. I have learned that emotional undercurrents always exist, even in rooms filled with logic and data. And if I fail to read them, I miss the signals that matter.

In my military years, reading people was often more critical than reading maps. In the corporate world, the same held true. Pressure has many faces; sometimes it shows up as defiance, sometimes as withdrawal, and sometimes as silence. Without emotional intelligence, it's easy to react to the behavior and miss the story behind it.

Leadership begins when we choose to see beyond the role someone plays and seek to understand their heart, their hurt, and their hope. That depth of understanding is what unlocks authentic connection. And when people feel understood, they begin to rise, not for the sake of a task, but for the strength of the relationship.

I saw this principle in action when organizations shifted from talking about people to truly investing in them. Is this simple idea: *Employee First, Customer Second.*

It might sound counterintuitive at first, especially in a world that's so focused on customer satisfaction and service metrics. But when you take a step back and really think about where value gets created, it becomes clear. That value is built in the space where employees and customers meet. It's in that everyday interaction, in that moment of service or support, where the company's reputation is actually formed.

So if that's the moment that matters most, then it makes sense to focus your energy on the people responsible for that moment. Which means the real work of leadership isn't pushing outcomes. It's building people. It's asking yourself, "What does this person need to succeed here?" And then following through. Encouragement, clarity, space to take initiative, room to fail without fear, the chance to ask tough questions, and still feel safe, those are the things that shape culture.

When leaders commit to putting employees first, those employees begin to take full ownership of the customer experience and put the customers first. It's not about reminding them what matters. They already know. Because someone made the effort to show them they matter first.

I've seen this play out in teams with no big budgets, no extra perks, and no shortcuts. Same people, same product, same customer, but something changed. The shift came from how they were led. Managers stopped focusing on control and started focusing on trust. And when that shift happens, it's felt. Customers notice it. Not because the process changed, but because the person behind the process showed up differently.

And here's what's worth remembering. Customers don't form loyalty from brand promises. They form loyalty from how your people treat them. And people give their best when they feel seen, supported, and believed in.

You can keep updating systems and refreshing strategy, but if the people doing the work don't feel valued, it will always fall short. When people care about where they work, that care flows outward. It shows up in the quality of effort, the tone in conversations, and the way challenges are handled.

A culture where people come first isn't built on policies. It's built on moments. And it starts when leaders stop looking up the chain for direction and start looking around at who they're responsible for. If you take care of the people creating the value, they'll take care of the people receiving it. It really is that simple.

There were moments I had to make tough calls, but how I delivered them made all the difference. Pausing before reacting. Asking instead of assuming. Offering space instead of demanding an explanation. These weren't techniques. They became leadership disciplines, habits rooted in emotional maturity.

And that maturity builds culture.

I've seen that when leaders bring presence and not just position into the room, it transforms how people respond. When a leader walks in with awareness, empathy, and clarity, the room doesn't tense; it aligns.

There's a pattern I began to notice: when teams are emotionally safe, feedback becomes honest. When feedback becomes honest, execution improves. And when execution improves, outcomes follow. But it starts with the tone set by leadership, one that balances accountability with understanding.

I always return to the principle that has grounded me across environments: People First, Mission Always. Emotional intelligence is what allows that philosophy to be lived, not just said. It helps us hold the mission with focus and our people with care, without compromising either.

The truth is, that empathy and emotional intelligence are not traits a leader either has or doesn't. They are practices. They are decisions made at the moment, again and again, to stay grounded in who we are while understanding what others need.

And the more we commit to those practices, the more we expand our capacity to lead, not from authority, but from connection. That connection is what allows us to move our people. To engage their belief before their behavior. To touch their hearts, before ever reaching for their hand.

Reflection and Action

Leadership is not a rank, it is a relationship. And the quality of that relationship is determined by the decisions we make every day in how we show up for others, and for ourselves.

Here are three reflection-based actions designed to slow you down just enough to check how you're leading, not in theory, but in the reality of your current relationships and culture:

1. The Silent Room Test

If your team gathered in a room without you, what would they say about your leadership presence?

Would they describe you as someone they can trust when things go wrong? Would your name spark a sense of safety or strategy? Openness, or tension? Sit with that question. If you're not sure, maybe it's time to ask them. Or better yet, show up in ways that speak for themselves.

2. The Inner Battle Journal

Over the next seven days, set aside five minutes at the end of each day to log one moment where your inner dialogue affected your outer behavior.

Did you lead with clarity or react to stress? Did you hold space for someone or rush through a conversation? What you'll start to notice isn't failure, but patterns. Patterns are the starting point of transformation.

3. The Empathy Audit

Pick three names: one peer, one junior, and one person you've unintentionally overlooked.

Now, answer: Do they know where they stand with you? When was the last time you engaged with them without an agenda? If you hesitate, use the next week to reconnect, genuinely, not formally. Not to give feedback. Just to listen. And watch how quickly trust begins to refill.

<u>Key Takeaways</u>

- **Leadership begins with presence, not position:** People follow those who show up, listen deeply, and stand steady in uncertainty.

- **Caring is about being consistent:** Real care means guiding with respect, correcting with dignity, and creating a space where people feel safe to rise.

- **Morale doesn't come from perks, it's built daily through clarity and trust:** It's the invisible force that drives resilience, initiative, and the will to go beyond what's required.

- **Great leaders clear the fog of past experiences:** One bad interaction shouldn't shape how you see the next person. Wipe the lens clean every time.

- **Before you can lead people, lead your mind:** Your mindset shapes how you show up for others. Leading yourself with clarity and belief sets the tone for everything else.

- **Trust is built in the ordinary, not just the exceptional:** It grows in how you show up every day, when you speak truth, follow through, and care for your people without drama.

- **Empathy is awareness, not indulgence:** It's tuning into what isn't said. When people feel understood, they engage from belief, not obligation.

- **Emotional safety fuels honest feedback and stronger execution:** Culture shifts when people no longer fear being real, and that shift begins with the leader's tone and presence.

Performance – The Discipline of Execution

When people feel seen, valued, and safe, they don't need to be pushed, they begin to move with purpose. That's the power of trust. But trust alone doesn't drive results. It creates the foundation. What happens next depends on clarity, consistency, and execution.

Caring is where leadership begins. But performance is where leadership is tested.

You can invest in people, build morale, and foster emotional safety, but if the mission stalls, leadership comes under pressure. Not from critics, but from within. Because deep down, every committed leader knows this: what you care about must eventually show in what you deliver.

This is where performance steps in, not as a call for speed, but for precision. Not as pressure to impress, but as discipline to follow through. A leader doesn't perform once. A leader performs every time it matters.

I've seen this both in command and in corporate corridors. Soldiers didn't need micromanagement. They needed clarity on the objective. And once they had that, they didn't wait for reminders. They took the ground. Similarly, in business, whether scaling a global function or leading through volatility, results came not from long meetings, but from focused action repeated over time.

The principle we lived by in uniform was simple: Selection and Maintenance of Aim. In simpler terms, get clear about the mission and refuse to blur that aim, no matter what. In tank operations, once the gun is locked on target, the stabilizer system ensures it stays locked, even if the tank has to change or adjust course due to battle conditions or terrain constraints. I used to think of that every time my team encountered turbulence in business. The strategy could shift. The plan could evolve. But the aim? That had to stay steady.

When I discovered the Four Disciplines of Execution (4DX) framework written by Chris McChesney, Jim Huling, and Sean Covey, it gave structure to something I had long practiced intuitively. Identifying what really matters, what they call the Wildly Important Goals, reminded me of our battlefield briefs: focus on what moves the mission. Then track lead measures, the small, daily actions that drive the big results. Display progress in a scoreboard that everyone can see. And most importantly, create a rhythm of ownership and accountability where commitments are visible, and execution becomes everyone's business.

That rhythm is what I brought with me when I transitioned from the war room to the boardroom. As I led international teams at NIIT, we anchored around a common objective. Each team knew exactly what their aim was. We built performance reviews that resembled after-action debriefs, rigorous but focused on growth. We measured what mattered. We celebrated small wins. And we stayed in the fight until the objective was met.

But performance is not about pressure. It is about clarity. It is about creating a culture where people know what is expected, why it matters, and how they will be supported in getting there. When people feel cared for, they dare more. They go beyond metrics. They begin to take ownership.

That's why I believe execution and empathy are not at odds. Without care, discipline becomes control. Without discipline, care becomes indulgence. The real art of high-performance leadership lies in holding both. I have always tried to be the kind of leader who sets the bar and then walks with the team as they reach it. And every time we've achieved something extraordinary, it was never because of individual brilliance; it was because of collective discipline.

I've learned that if I lose sight of the mission, I lose momentum. And if I lower the bar on consistency, I dilute the culture. That's not leadership.

So, the question I want to ask every leader is, *Are you locked onto your mission, or have you been swept up by the whirlwind?*

Because in the end, performance is not a one-time act. It is a decision we make every single day.

Encouraging High Performance in Teams

I have always believed that people don't perform for policies. They perform for people. No system, process, or incentive can outpace the power of a leader who knows how to create an environment that inspires belief. And once belief is in place, performance becomes personal.

Whether I was commanding soldiers or leading teams across 40 countries, one thing remained constant: people give their best when they feel seen, trusted, and valued. It's easy to talk about high-performance cultures. But culture doesn't live in slogans, it lives in behaviors. It lives in the way leaders show up, hold people accountable, and recognize their effort even when results take time.

In my military career, we were trained to operate with minimal margin for error. And yet, the most high-performing teams I led weren't the ones driven by fear, they were the ones anchored in mutual trust. Every tank commander, crew member, and soldier knew that feedback would come fast and straight, not to pull them down, but to raise the bar. That's what high-performing environments do: they lift people without letting standards fall.

When I moved into corporate leadership, I noticed something missing. Leaders often hesitated to offer feedback, fearing pushback or conflict. But what I've come to learn is this: silence kills performance. Feedback when it's timely, clear, and caring is the oxygen of growth. If I never tell my team where they're off track, I deny them the opportunity to get it right. And if I never tell them when they're doing well, I rob them of the fuel to keep going.

High performance isn't driven by pressure. It is driven by clarity, encouragement, and accountability. One of the most effective things I ever did with my team was introduce a rhythm of "execution huddles."

Short, focused check-ins where each person declared one meaningful action they would take to move the goal forward. And the next week, they reported back. No excuses. No stories. Just ownership.

There is a story that reminds me of how deeply a culture of accountability can shape performance without force. In 1998, Synovus Bank, a relatively unknown bank in Georgia, was named the best company to work for in America by Fortune Magazine. Their growth numbers were staggering. But when Dr. John Izzo asked their CEO about the secret behind their success, the answer was simple: love and responsibility. Synovus had a culture built around what they called "100/0." Every person was expected to take 100% responsibility for their performance and make zero excuses. It wasn't a slogan. It was lived every day. Whether it was showing up on time, owning service quality, or caring for colleagues, everyone understood that success was personal and collective. It wasn't about avoiding mistakes. It was about standing tall for what you could influence, without shifting blame. That kind of ownership created both resilience and pride. It turned expectations into habits and habits into culture.

This rhythm mirrored what I had seen in the 4 Disciplines of Execution (4DX), where focus on the wildly important goals, acting on lead measures, keeping a visible scoreboard, and creating a cadence of accountability becomes part of the culture. I didn't implement it as a framework. I lived it as a way of working. Over time, that rhythm built consistency, and consistency built momentum.

Recognition also played a huge part. I wasn't always big on grand awards. But I made it a habit to call out progress, especially when someone dared to challenge the status quo or took a tough call aligned with the mission. Recognition, when it's specific and sincere, becomes reinforcement. It says, "I see you. Keep going." That one sentence has kept more people in the game than any bonus could.

At NIIT, I had the opportunity to lead teams across diverse geographies and cultural landscapes. What stood out was how deeply the organization valued alignment, not just to goals, but to people. Planning was not treated as a top-down exercise. Instead, there was a conscious effort to engage individuals, understand what mattered to them, and connect those personal drivers to the mission. When people could see their own growth reflected in the direction we were moving, they didn't just perform, they took ownership. That sense of alignment made a measurable difference. It built commitment that wasn't dependent on deadlines or oversight, it was rooted in meaning.

Outside of NIIT, I noticed that this wasn't always the case. In some corporate environments, planning often happens in isolation, strategy gets designed in boardrooms without tapping into what truly motivates the people expected to execute it. While it would be unfair to generalize the corporate world, I've observed that when individuals feel excluded from the process, they also feel detached from the outcome. And when the mission doesn't resonate, performance becomes a task, not a commitment.

I've also seen how motivation tends to fade in environments where progress is invisible. It's rarely about laziness. More often, people lose energy because they can't see the impact of their work. That's where measurement makes all the difference. Not in the form of sterile dashboards, but through simple, visible scoreboards, tools that the team owns, updates, and celebrates together. When progress is seen, belief is sustained. And when belief is sustained, performance follows.

In my experience, three things consistently lift team performance:

- Freedom to act with clarity

- Frequent, honest feedback

- Recognition of effort, not just outcomes

And above all, a leader who holds the team to high standards because they believe they are worth it.

No team wakes up high-performing. They are built, breath by breath, by leaders who dare to care and discipline at the same time. My role, always, has been to bring that daring into the room. To say, "You're capable of more. Let's go find it."

That is how performance stops being a metric and starts becoming a mindset.

Strategic Alignment: Principles of War in Corporate Execution

Some of the most effective leadership tools I carried into the business world were not picked up in boardrooms. They came from the terrain of real missions, often in high-stakes conditions where every decision carried weight. The Indian Army instilled in me a habit of thinking and acting with structure, but never with rigidity. At the core of that approach were the Principles of War.

These principles were not theoretical constructs. They were the operating system for every mission I led, both in uniform and later in my corporate leadership journey. When I stepped into business, I didn't leave those principles behind. Instead, I adapted them. What I found was that they translated directly into driving execution, building alignment, and sustaining performance in any organization.

Let me share how I've applied each of these in both the operational and business world.

Selection and Maintenance of Aim

This is where it begins. Clarity of mission. A clear articulation of what success looks like. In every military operation, we ensured that every soldier knew the objective. Not through lengthy presentations or elaborate vision statements, but in a way that could be acted upon without hesitation.

In business, I noticed that a lot of teams lacked this kind of sharpness. Meetings were filled with movement, but not necessarily with alignment. At NIIT, whether we were working on the Chiphen Rigpel project in Bhutan or rolling out global learning programs, we started by defining our aim in simple, unambiguous terms. When the goal is well-defined, the strategy naturally aligns around it.

And once that aim is selected, it must be maintained with discipline. The distractions are many, and the temptation to chase new targets can dilute execution. I made it a point to reinforce the primary mission until it became second nature across teams.

Offensive Action

You cannot gain ground by sitting back. Initiative matters. The unit that moves first controls the tempo of engagement. That was drilled into us during operations, and it remains true in corporate settings.

I saw this play out clearly when we expanded into underserved markets. Take the Cloud Campus initiative across Indonesia, Vietnam, and Nigeria. The market conditions were not perfect. There were risks involved. But instead of waiting for a so-called "ideal" entry point, we moved with speed and intent. That ability to act rather than react gave us an edge. In most markets, early movers shape the conversation. They learn faster and adapt quicker.

In execution terms, waiting often creates more uncertainty than momentum. And leadership is not about watching from the sidelines. It is about stepping forward, even when the outcome is not fully guaranteed.

Offensive action isn't always about a head-on charge. Sometimes it's about choosing the right kind of attack for the situation. In one of our corporate campaigns, we structured the strategy across four fronts. We used a frontal attack to move directly into the market with strength through a blitz of visibility, targeted offers, and clear communication of our value. We used flank attacks to quietly exploit competitor gaps where their products or services were weaker. An envelopment attack helped us widen our presence across key locations and overwhelm the market with our product dominance. And where precision mattered, we adopted a guerrilla approach, making small, strategic moves in high-impact areas that shifted momentum over time.

Every piece of the plan focused on speed, adaptability, and winning ground one step at a time, rather than waiting for perfect conditions. It was a reminder that offensive action is not about rushing in blindly. It's about applying pressure smartly, at the right points, until the environment bends in your favor.

Cooperation

Missions are not accomplished in isolation. Teams that perform well do so because they act as one unit. Cooperation in the military meant synchronized action between units, often under high stress. There was no space for silos.

In the corporate world, I have seen many brilliant minds underperform simply because they were working in parallel, not in sync. When we rolled out educational programs across Latin America or South Africa, the initiative spanned multiple stakeholders, foreign ministries, local delivery teams, and internal curriculum experts. Success depended on all of them operating with shared clarity.

At NIIT, we built structures for cross-functional cooperation into the planning phase itself. Without it, execution would have been fragmented. Coordination creates confidence. When teams move in step, performance accelerates.

Concentration of Force and Economy of Effort

Resources are never unlimited. In operations, we were taught to concentrate force where it mattered most, and not to scatter effort across multiple fronts. That principle helped us win not by doing more, but by doing what mattered, where it mattered.

In business, the same logic applies. When we led initiatives like the scholarship rollout in Nigeria, we zeroed in on key regions and high-impact interventions. In a single year, we enrolled over sixty-three thousand students. That level of reach would not have been possible if we had spread ourselves thin. It came from focusing energy, talent, and resources where they could move the dial.

The same rule applies in budgeting. Instead of funding everything marginally, we backed high-impact programs with full force. That clarity allowed us to scale with conviction.

Flexibility

No matter how well you plan, conditions will change. The battlefield taught me that quickly. What saved us wasn't the plan; it was the ability to adapt while staying aligned with the mission.

In the corporate world, flexibility came from preparation, not improvisation. For instance, when we launched learning programs across the Maldives, we had to adapt constantly. Each island had different infrastructure, different limitations. Yet we delivered certifications to more than two thousand people across forty-two islands. That was possible only because the team had built strong feedback loops and stayed agile in how they responded.

True flexibility is built on mastering the basics. To hone systems, processes, and procedures to precision. It then gives you room to sense the situation, think clearly, act with speed, and renew the process to adapt to changing and fluid situations.

Simplicity

Complexity kills execution. In the field, a plan that required long explanations was a plan that would fail under stress. So we kept things simple. Clear. Actionable.

That habit carried over. I have often asked business leaders to explain their strategy in a few sentences. Most cannot. The strategy might be sound, but if it cannot be understood across the team, it will never be executed well.

When we were working in South Africa on school math labs across hundreds of institutions, or in China across several provinces & universities, we kept the plan lean and easy to communicate. That allowed ground-level educators and teams to move without constant clarification. Simplicity makes ownership easier. It eliminates doubt and shortens the time between decision and action.

These principles helped me execute when resources were limited, timelines were short, and conditions were unpredictable. They gave me a way to ground my leadership in action, not abstraction.

And I still rely on them when I work with teams today. Whether it's coaching senior executives or building performance cultures from scratch, these principles show up again and again. Not as buzzwords. But as practical disciplines that make execution sharper, faster, and more sustainable.

Leadership, in its truest sense, is not defined by how much you do. It is defined by what you choose to focus on and how consistently you move your team toward that objective.

The principles I learned in uniform did not belong to war. They belonged to leadership. They taught me to think clearly, act decisively, and deliver outcomes that matter.

And they still do.

Daring to Deliver: Cultivating the Courage to Perform

Performance is not the absence of fear. It is the decision to act despite it. If there's one thing I've learned in over four decades of leading people, whether in high-stakes operations, international business expansions, or deep coaching conversations, it is this: the greatest enemy of execution is not incompetence. It's hesitation.

People often think performance is about skill. And yes, skill matters. But when I've looked closely at what has moved teams from average to extraordinary, it has never been just capability, it has been courage. The willingness to stretch, to challenge assumptions, to move forward when the outcome isn't guaranteed. That is the kind of daring that sustains real performance.

There was a phrase I once heard in a strategy meeting: "Let's play it safe." I remember pausing. Looking around the room. And asking a simple question, "When has safety ever led to transformation?"

The kind of performance I've pursued all my life, whether in the army or in the corporate world, has never been about maintenance. It has always been about momentum. And momentum demands movement. Sometimes bold. Often uncomfortable. Always deliberate.

After I transitioned from military command to business leadership, I found myself in rooms where the language was different but the hesitation was familiar. On the battlefield, fear at times shows up as indecision. In the boardroom, it shows up as a delay. In both worlds, daring leaders are the ones who decide. Who speaks up? Who acts, not recklessly, but with clarity.

At NIIT, when we were looking to enter unfamiliar international markets, there was always the easy path to wait for better data, a more "mature" environment, and lower risk. But I had seen enough in my life to know that waiting rarely breeds readiness. We chose to act. To move with calculated boldness. To test, adapt, and respond. That's when real breakthroughs started to happen. The kind that scale teams, open new regions, and rewrite performance norms.

In leadership, we often talk about building high-performance cultures. What we don't talk about enough is how to cultivate courage. It takes the kind of courage it takes to speak an uncomfortable truth. To own a failure publicly. To admit when we're stuck and ask for help. These are the moments that create safety in a team. And when people feel safe, they stop holding back.

I've always encouraged the teams I've led to take on a "no retreat" mindset. That doesn't mean throwing caution aside. It means removing the quiet fallback plans that give people an excuse to hold back.

One example that's stayed with me for years is what Alexander the Great did when he landed in Persia. His army had crossed the sea and faced a force much larger than their own. Most leaders would have reinforced their escape route. Alexander did the opposite. He ordered the ships to be burned. There would be no going back. His men had to fight forward. And they did. That one decision changed everything. It created urgency, clarity, and focus. I've seen this play out in business, too. The moment teams decide there's no side door, no soft landing, and no Plan B, they show up differently. Complacency fades. Effort becomes intense. People begin to fight for the mission like it's theirs, because it is.

That same spirit underpins the 4DX principle of Wildly Important Goals. Choosing what really matters is not a tactical decision. It is a daring one. Because to prioritize one thing is to de-prioritize many others. And that requires courage, the courage to say no to the noise, and yes to the one mission that will truly move the needle.

It's the same with lead measures. When you commit to daily behaviors that shape future outcomes, you're taking a leap of faith. You don't have instant results. You don't have a guarantee. But you choose to believe that disciplined action will compound. That belief itself is an act of daring.

When coaching senior leaders today, I often ask them: "What's the one decision you're avoiding?" That question usually unlocks more than any strategic framework. Because behind every plateau is usually a pause that fear created. Once we move through that fear, performance follows.

My own career has been defined by moments where hesitation could have taken root. But I had lived through a time when I didn't have the luxury of retreat. That memory is enough. I don't need to relive the moment, but I carry its weight. It reminds me that when you no longer give yourself the option to withdraw, you discover reserves of strength you didn't know you had.

High performance, then, isn't just about structure. It is about spirit. You can install dashboards and design KPIs. But without courage, none of that sustains. Teams that consistently deliver are not the ones with the most polished plans, they're the ones with the deepest belief. Belief in the mission. That belief gets tested most when the terrain is unknown.

When I served as a Senior Military Observer with the United Nations in Cambodia, one of my responsibilities was to lead patrols deep into the thick, treacherous jungles of Battambang province, a region still haunted by the shadows of the Khmer Rouge.

These were not routine patrols. The forests we navigated were heavily mined, with no reliable records or maps. Every step forward was a calculated risk. There were no guarantees. Only resolve.

Our mission was to reach hidden Khmer Rouge encampments for negotiations aimed at disarmament and reintegration, efforts crucial to the fragile peace process. These journeys demanded more than physical endurance; they called for calm amidst chaos, moral courage, and deep trust in both the people beside me and the purpose ahead.

There were moments of deep silence in those jungles, not out of serenity, but because fear itself had to be subdued. We couldn't afford panic. We had to lead steadily, deliberately, and with presence.

Looking back, I realize those missions were not just about reaching coordinates or fulfilling a UN mandate. They were about leading from the front when the path was unclear, both literally and metaphorically. They taught me that leadership isn't just about the known terrain; it's about walking into uncertainty with clarity, humility, and a fire that doesn't flicker in the face of fear.

So if you're trying to shift the performance of your team, ask yourself, not just what they know, but what they're afraid of. And ask yourself as a leader: Am I modeling comfort, or am I modeling courage?

Because performance without daring is compliance.

But performance fueled by courage? That becomes a conviction.

And conviction delivers.

Reflection and Action

Over the years, I've learned that performance doesn't need more pressure; it needs more purpose. More clarity. More commitment. More daring. I've seen top-tier leaders get stuck not because they lacked competence, but because they lost sight of the mission or became too comfortable managing instead of delivering.

What has always helped me stay anchored, whether in the field or in the boardroom, is pausing to ask the right questions.

So take this moment to reflect. Not to judge, but to realign.

1) Ask Yourself:

- What is the Wildly Important Goal that truly deserves your team's energy right now?

- Is your team tracking what they can influence each day, or only measuring what's already done?

- Have you crafted a compelling scoreboard?

- Do you hold people accountable from a place of care and belief, or from habit and hierarchy?

2) Personal Pause

Where are you hesitating?
What conversation have you been avoiding?
What standard have you quietly let slip?

Remember, when performance slips quietly, results disappear loudly.

I often return in my mind to a moment, one I've already shared earlier, that reminded me what it means to finish the mission despite pain, uncertainty, and fear. That day left scars, yes, but it also left something more enduring: a resolve to never let my circumstances speak louder than my convictions. That resolve has guided every decision I've made, from how I lead, how I coach, and how I hold myself accountable.

Performance is personal (ownership) before it ever becomes professional. It begins in the mind, travels through action, and shows up in results.

3) Action Steps:

- Choose One Mission: Clarify your team's Wildly Important Goal and eliminate the noise.

- Make It Measurable: Define 2–3 lead measures your team can act on consistently.

- Build in the Rhythm: Set up weekly huddles that focus on ownership, not oversight.

If I could leave you with one thing, it's this: Results aren't built in strategy meetings. They're built in moments of decision. The kind where you choose to focus, to act, to own.

So whatever your mission, hold it with steady hands. Set the pace. Burn the mental ships. Dare to deliver.

Because performance is never about doing more. It's about doing what matters, again and again, with clarity and courage.

<u>Key Takeaways</u>

- **Performance reveals itself in what gets repeated, not what gets announced:** Clarity, rhythm, and accountability matter more than pressure; leaders deliver not once, but every time it counts.

- **Discipline without care feels like control; care without discipline drifts.** High performance is sustained when standards are upheld with belief, not with fear.

- **People perform for belief, not policies:** When teams feel seen and trusted, performance shifts from obligation to ownership.

- **Execution thrives on simplicity and focus:** The clearest goal, acted on consistently, outpaces even the smartest strategy left unexecuted.

- **Feedback is not a risk, it's a responsibility:** Honest, timely feedback fuels growth. Silence, on the other hand, stalls it.

- **Accountability builds momentum when it's shared, not imposed:** Weekly check-ins, visible scoreboards, and ownership conversations turn strategy into traction.

- **Courage is the real engine behind performance:** Results follow when leaders stop waiting for perfect conditions and start acting from conviction.

- **Sustained excellence comes from alignment, not effort alone:** When personal drivers meet a clear mission, performance becomes personal, and they take ownership – that's when people go beyond the brief.

Chapter
05

Legacy – Leadership That Outlives You

"Carve your name on hearts, not tombstones. A legacy is etched into the minds of others and the stories they share about you."

– Shannon L. Alder

The first time I truly understood the meaning of legacy was when I found myself staring at the sky from the ground beside my tank, the weight of two and a half decades in uniform pressing into the cold beneath me. That moment didn't feel like an end. It felt like a handover. From what I had achieved to what I would build. From success to significance.

Legacy is often mistaken for applause after a job well done. It isn't. It's the echo of who you were when the room falls silent. It's found in the questions people ask long after you've stepped away: *What will people say about the way you led? What story will they carry forward? What values did you leave behind in them?*

Over the years, I've learned that leadership isn't measured in trophies, titles, or time served. It's measured in transfer. Our lives are shaped. In the standards that continue when you are no longer the one enforcing them. That's why I say *there is no success without a successor.* If your ideas, convictions, and principles didn't take root in someone else, then they end with you. And that becomes self-centered leadership.

One of the finest examples of legacy I've witnessed wasn't in a formal structure or institution, but in a soldier. Captain Vikram Batra. The fact that we still speak of him today, that a mountain carries his name, and that his actions inspired generations, is proof that legacy doesn't wait for retirement. It begins with every decision you make. Every life you impact. Every standard you raise.

When I moved from commanding tanks to building business strategy, and later to coaching leaders across boardrooms, I carried forward one principle: People First – Mission Always. I've repeated it so often that some may think it's a slogan. It isn't. It's a decision I've made again and again, across continents, cultures, crises. It has shaped the way I listen, lead, coach, and pass the baton. I've seen what happens when leaders hold too tightly to authority. Nothing grows. Legacy is built when you trust others enough to carry it forward.

Leadership that outlives you is built on how you make people feel seen, valued, and stretched. It's not built through authority, but through alignment. Not through power, but through purpose. And above all, it's not something you earn in the end. It's something you build with intention, every single day.

I often ask leaders I coach a question they don't always expect: *If your career ended tomorrow, what would people say you stood for? Not your résumé. Not your projects. You. What values would they associate with you? What habits? What attitudes?*

These questions aren't for reflection at the end of a career. They are meant to be asked while you're in the thick of it. Because legacy isn't a eulogy. It's a mirror.

It isn't sculpted in stone, it's written into people.

And it begins with a decision: *What kind of leader do you want the next generation to thank you for being?*

Building a Leadership Legacy

When people speak of legacy, they often think in terms of monuments, medals, or names on plaques. That has never resonated with me. For me, legacy is far less visible and far more enduring. It lives in the character of those you've influenced, in the decisions they make when you're no longer in the room, and in the stories they tell when your name comes up.

I've always believed that your actions write your eulogy long before anyone else does.

During my time in uniform, I saw leadership up close, in the quiet decisions of commanding officers, in the courage of junior leaders, in the small acts of care that never made it into citation reports. Those were the moments that stayed. They reminded me that the weight of a leader's influence isn't measured with awards, during parades, or promotions. It's measured when those under your command carry forward your values long after you've passed the baton.

Legacy doesn't begin at the end. It begins with how you show up every day. I've seen leaders become so fixated on milestones and titles that they forget the larger question: *What will remain when I step away?*

This is where ethical leadership plays a decisive role. You can delegate tasks. You can even outsource strategies. But you cannot delegate integrity. That's personal. And it shows up in the way you treat people when no one is watching, in how you handle power, and in the standards you refuse to lower even when it costs you comfort.

There was a time in my transition from military to civilian life when I questioned my own value. I had no corporate designation, no MBA, no business jargon to offer. What I had was something else: clarity of purpose, an ingrained sense of service, and a belief that leadership wasn't about elevation but about impact.

As William James once said, *"The greatest use of a life is to spend it on something that will outlast it."* That idea shaped how I approached my second career. I wasn't looking to build success. I was looking to build something that would stand when I stepped aside.

One of the most fulfilling parts of my journey has been mentoring high-potential leaders. Many of them came with sharp resumes and sharper ambitions. What they needed was not more goals. They needed grounding. And that came from asking the right questions. What do you want to be remembered for? What sentence would you want others to speak when they reflect on your leadership?

These aren't easy questions. But they are necessary.

Legacy, to me, means that someone I led once stands taller because of something they learned through our interaction. It means a team continues to operate with values I instilled, even when I'm no longer part of the chain of command. That's when you know you've left something behind that matters.

I've coached leaders across sectors. Some have walked into the room with the weight of power on their shoulders. Others have come searching for it. The ones who make the greatest impact are those who understand that their legacy will not be defined by how high they climbed, but by how far their influence reached.

It isn't about who reports to you. It's about who grows because of you.

And that's where mentorship becomes more than a professional courtesy. It becomes a responsibility. If we don't prepare others to lead better than us, we're not leading. We're preserving power, not multiplying it. As Steve Jobs put it, *"My job is not to be easy on people. My job is to make them better."* That is what real succession looks like. Not handovers. Growth.

Over time, I've learned that legacy embeds itself in culture when your actions match your values consistently, especially under pressure. I've seen it in field units and executive boardrooms alike. When a leader listens well, acts decisively, and honors their word, those around them pick up more than strategies. They absorb a standard.

And they pass it on.

You don't need a plaque to tell you that your leadership made an impact. You'll see it when someone you coached makes a call that reflects your principles. You'll feel it when they hold the line under pressure, not because you asked them to, but because it's what they believe is right.

Legacy isn't a reward. It's the residue of who you are when you're fully present, consistently, without seeking attention for it.

It's not built into the big speeches. It's built on the small decisions. The ones that nobody claps for, but everyone remembers.

That's how you build a legacy. Not in titles. In people.

Legacy in Military, Corporate, and Personal Leadership

Military Perspective

The military doesn't talk about legacy. It lives it. You don't have to look for succession plans or vision statements to find continuity in the armed forces. It's built into the system. The moment a young cadet steps onto the parade ground, he steps into a stream of values that has been flowing for decades. Discipline, honor, duty, these aren't phrases we wore on our sleeves. They were the standard we protected with our conduct.

At the Indian Military Academy, the Chetwode Motto wasn't a recital. It was a pledge. We learned early that real leadership begins when you put the welfare of your men above your own. That simple idea shaped every command decision I ever made. It taught me that authority can be assigned, but respect has to be earned. And it's earned through consistency, fairness, and moral courage.

One of the most powerful examples I've seen of legacy in the military was during my time in The Scinde Horse and later commanding of 46 Armoured Regiment. The regiment didn't operate on fear or hierarchy. It ran on trust. Young officers looked up to their seniors not because they shouted louder, but because they showed up when it counted. That is what lived on. When those juniors moved up in rank, they remembered how they were led. And they passed that standard forward.

I still remember when I was commanding Alpha Squadron of 46 Armoured Regiment, between 1989 and 1992, a tightly bonded, fourteen-tank sub-unit. Those years remain etched in memory not just for what we achieved, but for what was quietly set in motion.

From the outset, we found our rhythm in what I came to call relaxed efficiency. Everything from operations, to training and sports, to administration, and equipment was executed with care and precision, but without the pressure of micromanagement. There was discipline, certainly, but not at the cost of initiative. The intent was simple: to build a culture that didn't rely on constant supervision, but rather thrived on internal ownership. I wanted the squadron to run not on fear or compliance, but on pride. Not through orders, but through identity.

And it worked.

We went on to win three consecutive inter-squadron championships. That in itself was gratifying. But what followed taught me something far deeper about leadership. Long after I moved on, Alpha Squadron continued to win, Alpha Squadron retained the championship for the next three years as well, and went on to win nine out of the eleven years that followed. What had started as a rhythm became a tradition. What began as a goal became a standard.

That's when I truly understood what it means to leave behind a legacy. Not one measured by your presence, but by what endures in your absence.

True legacy lives not in trophies or timelines, but in people. In the systems you shape, the culture you nurture, and the values you embed quietly and steadily into the DNA of a unit. It is not built through control, but through belief. Not imposed, but inherited.

Alpha Squadron's enduring success was never about one individual. It was about collective ownership. A sense of identity that each generation passed on to the next, not as an expectation, but as a given.

And in that, I saw the purest form of leadership: *To light a flame that others choose to carry forward, long after you've stepped aside.*

During my United Nations assignments, I worked with personnel from thirty-three countries. Many of us had never trained together. Some had conflicting styles and doctrines. But we found common ground in shared purpose. That is what legacy feels like, when values carry more weight than nationalities or titles. It confirmed for me that effective leadership doesn't arise from command, it grows from connection. As Robin Sharma once said, *"Leadership is not about a title or a designation. It's about impact, influence, and inspiration."*

The military also taught me something that I didn't understand fully at the time: that you're not building a legacy for yourself. You're building it into others. It's the way your men speak of you when you're not in the tent. It's the culture they sustain long after your posting order has come through. That's when you know the legacy is working. It's moving without you.

Corporate Perspective

When I moved from the war room to the boardroom, I carried my principles with me. I wasn't fluent in business speak. I didn't walk in with an MBA or a resume filled with quarterly wins. What I brought was something else: clarity, discipline, and a firm belief that people are the mission.

At NIIT, I led business across forty countries. The complexity was staggering: different markets, different regulations, different cultures. What kept us grounded was the clarity of purpose. I had seen how clarity in mission works in the military. I applied the same mindset here. Set the mission. Communicate it well. Then reinforce it with every decision.

We didn't need posters to remind people of our values. We embedded them in how we operated. When we built educational ecosystems in Bhutan, South Africa, Nigeria, and the Maldives, amongst others, we weren't chasing numbers. We were investing in people. Thousands of learners gained access to skill development programs that opened new doors for them. That, to me, is long-term success: creating systems that continue to deliver impact even after you've stepped away.

At the core of that impact was mentorship. I worked with leaders across levels, not to hand them tactics, but to pass on thought patterns. Real succession doesn't happen when someone can replicate your strategy. It happens when they can make decisions with the same integrity. As John Maxwell put it, *"Success is when I add value to myself. Significance is when I add value to others."*

Corporate legacy has little to do with the title. Titles fade. Legacy survives in cultures, in ways of thinking, and in how teams treat each other under pressure. If the spirit leaves when the leader exits, then the culture was never real to begin with.

One of the partners I worked with at Deloitte modeled this perfectly. He didn't talk about leadership. He built leaders. He made sure every interaction left the other person clearer, stronger, and more self-aware. I saw how he multiplied trust across the organization. That's what inspired me to ask myself: Who am I raising to carry forward what I believe in?

That's the question I now ask every leader I coach. Legacy isn't what you do. It's what you've influenced others to do without you.

Personal Leadership and Coaching

When I transitioned to coaching, I realized that personal legacy is the most invisible yet the most impactful. You don't always see the results of your coaching immediately. But if you've done it right, the leaders you've worked with will grow in ways that reflect the values you planted in them.

Over the years, I've coached more than ten thousand individuals. I've seen firsthand how clarity, humility, and emotional honesty change not just the leader but the culture they're part of. As Maya Angelou said, "People will forget what you said, people will forget what you did, but people will never forget how you made them feel." In leadership, that emotional memory is your signature.

The "Inside-Out" work I do with clients focuses on one core idea: legacy is not created at the end of a journey. It's created in every small interaction along the way. Every leader leaves a trail in conversations, decisions, and daily behavior. The strongest legacies I've seen are not built in power meetings. They're built in moments of clarity, candor, and care.

When a former client calls years later to share that a team member quoted one of our sessions back to them, I know the values have stuck. That's the mark of lasting leadership. You don't need applause to know you've made an impact. You'll see it reflected in how people lead when no one is watching.

As a leader, the question isn't whether you're building a legacy. You are. The only real question is: what kind?

Reflection and Action

A legacy isn't formed by accident. It's built choice by choice, day by day. These three assessments will help you evaluate where you are in your leadership journey and whether what you're building will truly outlive you.

These aren't for ticking boxes. They're meant to slow you down, shift your lens, and make the abstract feel real.

1. The Mirror Conversation

Stand in front of a mirror. Look yourself in the eye and say, out loud:

"I am remembered as a leader who…"

Now say the first five words that come naturally to you. Don't edit. Don't refine. Just speak.

Then ask yourself:

- Would you follow someone with that legacy?

- Would your team feel proud to say those words about you?

- Is this what you want to echo long after you've moved on?

This is a confrontation with self, not a performance. Honesty is where legacy begins.

2. The Invisible Impact List

Write down five people whose growth you've influenced in the last two years.

Now write what changed for them because of your presence, not your position.

Be specific. Did someone speak up more? Take a risk? Begin mentoring others? Handle adversity with more strength?

Now reflect:

- How did you shape that transformation?

- Was your influence intentional, or incidental?

Leadership legacy often leaves no signature, but it's felt in the courage, clarity, and confidence others carry forward because you were there.

3. The Values Transfer Checklist

Write down your three non-negotiable values as a leader. Then ask yourself:

- Who knows these values, not because I said them, but because I've lived them?

- Who demonstrates them consistently, because they learned them by observing me?

- Who could name them if I asked them today?

"The legacy you leave is the life you lead."

– Stephen Covey

Leadership doesn't end when the role does. Your actions, your character, and the standard you uphold will echo far beyond your presence, in how people think, how they behave, and how they lead others.

I'm reminded of a story I shared often during my command of 46 Armoured Regiment. It began as a simple anecdote in briefings and conversations, but over time, it became a metaphor, a battle cry, and eventually, a part of the Regiment's living memory. We called it Chal Chamki.

In Hindi, chal means "go," and Chamki was the name of a spirited, agile horse. Together, they performed in one of the most demanding equestrian disciplines called "tent pegging". This cavalry sport was considered a crucible of discipline, coordination, and mutual trust.

The event required the rider to strike four ground targets in rapid succession, first with a lance, then a sword, followed by a bayonet, and finally, with bare hands. The targets were small wooden pegs, barely visible at full gallop. The challenge wasn't only in the weapons. It was in the alignment between rider and horse, mind and muscle, instinct and intention.

Success in tent pegging came down to three things: focus, direction, and speed.

- **Focus** meant locking in on each target with complete clarity, ignoring the blur of motion, pressure, or fear.

- **Direction** was about unwavering commitment; every stride needed purpose.

- **Speed** had to be controlled; without discipline, momentum would scatter the mission.

And then came the war cry: "Chal Chamki!"

It rang out in rhythm, a declaration of belief, not command. The horse responded out of trust. The rider believed in Chamki, and Chamki answered that belief.

That mutual confidence turned a high-risk sport into a moment of complete alignment. Even today, many in the Regiment remember that story not as a performance, but as a reminder of what it takes to move forward with conviction and unity.

In time, Chal Chamki became a reminder of what it means to act with unity, clarity, and momentum. Even today, many in the Regiment remember that call. It lives on as a quiet standard, reminding us that achievement, whether in combat, leadership, or life, requires more than effort. It demands alignment.

The story was never just about a horse or a rider. It was about trust in motion. A partnership fueled by clarity of purpose, sharpened through repetition, and carried forward by belief.

In Chal Chamki, we found a metaphor for everything we stood for:

To focus without distraction.
To move with a direction.
To surge with speed, united in voice, purpose, and spirit.

Every decision is a message. Every conversation is a signal. And every moment is either reinforcing your values or eroding them. You don't need to wait for a title to begin. You've already started. The only question is, what are you building?

Lead today in a way that someone will one day say, *"I am who I am because of the way they led."*

That is legacy.

<u>Key Takeaways</u>

- **Legacy isn't what follows you, it's what continues through others:** It lives in how people lead when you're no longer in the room, not in what you once achieved.

- **Leadership that ends with you is incomplete:** Legacy begins when what you stand for is built into others and not held by you alone.

- **What you model gets remembered more than what you teach:** Your consistency, especially under pressure, sets the standard others carry forward.

- **Mentorship is responsibility:** Legacy is built when you intentionally grow others to lead with clarity, not copy your style.

- **Titles fade; values echo:** The culture you shape, the way people treat each other, and the standards you uphold, those last.

- **Legacy is a daily decision, not a retirement reflection:** It's formed in how you show up, listen, correct, and coach, long before anyone thanks you.

- **Ethical leadership leaves the deepest imprint:** What you won't compromise, even when no one's watching, becomes your quiet but lasting contribution.

- **Your story becomes someone else's compass:** Every time a former colleague holds the line because of something you lived, not said, you've built a legacy.

Chapter

06

The Spirit of Inspirational Leadership

What do people hold on to when they think of a leader?

People rarely remember the awards, roles, fancy presentations, or public praise. They remember how a leader made them feel in uncertain moments, the steady tone in a difficult meeting, the willingness to pause and listen when everyone else was rushing past, and the decisions they made when no one was there to clap or comment.

That's where leadership begins. Not in job titles or press releases, but in choices made quietly, especially when it would be easier to step away.

Through the years, whether in the military or the corporate world, I've come to believe that what truly defines a leader is their consistency. Not perfection. Not always having the answer. But a certain steadiness. A way of showing up that doesn't change with the room. A kind of presence that says, "You can count on me," without needing to say it out loud.

I've known leaders who had all the right skills on paper, but something was missing. They were smart, sharp, and experienced. But when pressure showed up, their direction shifted because they hadn't taken the time to figure out what they stood for. They hadn't done that inner work. And when things got loud, they got pulled in.

Then there were others. Leaders who didn't have big titles or grand speeches, but who held firm. They didn't chase attention. They didn't change their tone when someone important walked in. They were grounded. And people noticed. Not because they demanded respect, but because they had earned it quietly over time.

I've come to believe that leadership doesn't grow out of a single trait. It builds over time, through the way you hold four things in balance. Passion. People. Performance. And Legacy. These aren't separate categories. They're connected. When one is off, the others feel it.

There were seasons in my life where delivery took over everything else. And others where people dynamics became so intense, I barely had room to breathe. Sometimes, I found myself looking too far ahead and missing what was in front of me. Each time, I had to stop and ask, "What's slipping? What needs attention now?"

That check-in helped. Because these four areas don't stay even on their own. They need to be watched, adjusted, and sometimes re-learned. And it's not always easy. But the leaders who stay with it are the ones who leave something behind that lasts.

"People First, Mission Always." Those four words have guided how I've led across different seasons. In war rooms and boardrooms. In coaching sessions and classrooms. It's a daily decision. A way to remind myself that the people I lead matter more than the plans I make. And that the mission deserves my best, even when it feels like the odds are against it.

You don't need to wait for a promotion to lead this way. You don't need a bigger team or more attention. What you need is to be clear about what matters to you, and to let that clarity shape how you lead when no one's watching.

Leadership isn't built in loud moments. It's built in the quiet ones. When the easier path is right there, but you choose the harder one because you know it's the right call.

That's the spirit this chapter is focused on. Not a model. Not a theory. But a way of living and leading that keeps Passion, People, Performance, and Legacy from pulling away from each other.

It's in that balance that your leadership begins to feel real. Not just to others. But to you.

Tying Together Passion, People, Performance, and Legacy

Leadership isn't built on frameworks alone. It holds steady when the day-to-day gets hard, when people are uncertain, and when pressure builds. Over time, I've come to rely on four anchors that help me stay centered: Passion, People, Performance, and Legacy. Each one shapes how you show up. But when they connect, they give depth to who you are as a leader. And when one starts to slip, it doesn't take long for the others to feel it.

Passion is what lights the fuse. It's the reason you show up early without being asked. It's the reason you raise your hand when something feels off, even if no one else does. In uniform, passion shaped everything from how we trained, how we prepared, to how we showed up. No one needed reminders. The mission carried its own weight. That kind of clarity didn't leave when I stepped into boardrooms or began working with leadership teams. It showed up in different clothes. But the fire stayed the same. I've met leaders with all the right credentials, the sharpest strategy, and strong resumes. What they missed was that inner drive. Their teams noticed. Passion doesn't need a microphone, but it needs to be present. People can tell when you care.

And people do notice. That's where leadership gets tested. People are what give leadership its meaning. A plan will guide a team, but it won't hold them together. People follow people, not just charts and targets. Across several organizations, I've seen a pattern emerge. Leaders walk in with well-written strategies, solid metrics, and clear timelines. On paper, it all lines up. But what's often missing is connection. People want to feel part of something that respects their presence, not just their productivity.

Something shifts when leaders start asking better questions. Instead of "Are we on track?" they ask, "What do you need from me right now?" and "What are we missing?" When that shift happens, the room starts to breathe easier. People step in with more openness. Meetings turn into conversations, and feedback becomes useful. The mission becomes shared, not imposed.

That kind of partnership is what makes execution meaningful. Which brings me to performance. This is where everything begins to show. Passion and people build energy. But without performance, the energy goes nowhere. I've worked with global teams across sectors, and the same principle applies everywhere. Sustainable results don't come from pressure. They come from rhythm and readiness. In every leadership role I've held, whether overseeing an international education business or coaching executives, I've focused on setting expectations that are clear, consistent, and respected.

Teams need a rhythm they can trust. Not perfection. Not fear. Rhythm. When people know what they're working toward, how progress is measured, and why it matters, they take ownership. They start showing up with solutions, not just updates. I've seen teams with strong intent struggle because their process was scattered. That's where leadership steps in, not to micromanage, but to realign.

Performance isn't about pushing harder every time. Some of the most effective teams I've worked with knew when to pause. They knew how to self-correct before someone else had to step in. I've coached leadership teams who once viewed performance reviews as checkboxes. Over time, those sessions became spaces for real accountability and ownership. And more importantly, for coaching. That's the shift. When people start seeing performance not as pressure, but as preparation, you know the culture is turning a corner.

Now we come to Legacy. It doesn't speak often, but when it does, it carries weight. Legacy isn't found in closing remarks or farewell speeches. It's found in how your team behaves when you're not around. I've often asked leaders one question: What will stay when you leave? Not which reports or dashboards, but which values? Which habits? How will your name live in a decision, in a culture, in a story someone tells down the line?

Some of the strongest legacies I've seen weren't crafted with slogans. They were built through quiet consistency. A leader who refused to take a shortcut. A manager who owned a tough call so the team wouldn't carry it. A senior leader who chose to mentor quietly, with no need for credit. These moments don't get logged in performance systems, but they shape the memory of leadership. Often, they become the example others follow without even realizing it.

In many coaching conversations with senior leaders, one theme keeps coming back. There's a decision to be made between chasing quick wins and building long-term strength. Short-term paths bring fast results. But they often leave teams stretched thin and disconnected. The alternative feels slower at first. But it brings people along. And when people are part of the journey, the results don't fade.

That's when I invite leaders to pause and ask a different question. Not about numbers or timelines. Something simpler. What kind of path would you want the person who comes after you to follow? That question often brings more clarity than a spreadsheet. Because legacy isn't formed once the work is done. It takes shape in every trade-off, in every decision where the easier route is available and you choose not to take it.

When Passion, People, Performance, and Legacy integrate, leadership starts to feel grounded. It becomes something you lead with inspiration, confidence, and clarity. And when you're leading with the right intent and purpose, it doesn't wear you down. It strengthens you.

Some days, one part will demand more than the others. You may find yourself consumed with delivery. Or deep in people dynamics. Or thinking about what you're building for the future. That's part of the process. The goal isn't to hold all four perfectly at all times. It's to be honest about where you're leaning and willing to rebalance when it matters.

The leaders who build cultures that outlive them aren't the ones who focus on one strength. They're the ones who stayed with the work, even when one piece got uncomfortable.

They knew that leadership was never about holding on to control. It was about knowing what to carry, when to carry it, and who you're carrying it for.

Protecting What Matters When it's the Hardest

When everything is aligned, passion driving your purpose, people carrying the mission, performance reflecting the preparation, and legacy taking root quietly, leadership feels inspiring and steady. But keeping that alignment intact is where the real work begins.

It's one thing to stand by your values in a controlled environment. It's another to hold them when circumstances stretch you, when timelines get tighter, and when expectations keep shifting. I've worked with leaders who started with clarity but found themselves pulled in different directions over time. Not because they stopped caring. But because the noise around them got louder than the voice within.

Staying true to your mission and values doesn't happen by chance. It requires constant attention. Because pressure will always try to blur your edges.

One of the most common challenges I've seen is what I call value fatigue. It doesn't happen overnight. It creeps in quietly, through repeated exposure to grey zones. A deadline that encourages compromise. A board decision that rewards the wrong behavior. A situation where silence seems safer than standing up. These aren't dramatic failures. They're slow shifts. And when left unchecked, they begin to chip away at what once felt non-negotiable.

What keeps values intact over time is not idealism. It's design. Leaders who sustain their integrity usually have clear habits in place that help them check themselves regularly. They don't leave their ethical judgment to mood or convenience. They create conditions that help them stay grounded, a sounding board they trust, a daily practice of reflection, and a clear internal contract they won't trade, even under stress.

I've seen this across both military and corporate environments. In high-pressure roles, the temptation to abandon the long view in favor of quick wins can be strong. Especially when rewards seem tied to short-term delivery. That's when the difference between personal ambition and professional purpose becomes critical. Leaders who tie their identity to results alone begin to bend their values when results become uncertain. But those who stay anchored to a mission, something bigger than personal gain, tend to hold their shape longer. They may feel the strain, but they don't lose their direction.

This is where "People First, Mission Always" becomes more than a motto. It becomes a standard. When you're in a position of responsibility, people are watching how you make decisions. Not the easy ones. The ones that require trade-offs. Your team sees when you pause to ask if something is right before asking if it's allowed. They notice when you own a hard truth instead of avoiding it. And they remember how you acted when doing the right thing came with a cost.

Leaders who stay true to their mission over time are rarely reactive. They tend to operate with clarity. And that clarity often comes from preparation. Just like a soldier doesn't think twice about where to move under fire, ethical leaders don't freeze when tension rises. They've trained for that moment, not in drills, but in daily behavior. They've made enough small decisions with integrity that the big ones feel like a natural extension.

This kind of consistency isn't always seen in the spotlight, but it stands out in critical moments. I'm reminded of how Johnson & Johnson responded during the Tylenol crisis in the early 80s. Seven lives were lost. There was fear, confusion, and intense public scrutiny. The pressure to protect the brand must have been immense. But the company didn't wait for legal direction or for blame to be confirmed. They acted. Millions of bottles were pulled from shelves, production was halted, and they began redesigning their packaging for safety. The most striking part wasn't the scale of the recall, but the speed and clarity of their response. It showed that their values were real, not promotional. Those decisions weren't made because someone told them what to do. They were made because the company already knew what it stood for. When that kind of clarity exists before the crisis, the response becomes instinctive.

One practice I often recommend is to write down your non-negotiables. Not your goals. Your lines. What are the boundaries you won't cross? Write them when things are calm, so you don't have to think about them when they're not. Because in the heat of delivery, reflection gets crowded out. When you're tired or cornered, you will fall back on the values you've rehearsed, not the ones you've only spoken about.

Another tool that works is having an accountability circle. This doesn't have to be formal. A few people who know your core, who can call you out without posturing, and who care enough to ask, "Are you still being the leader you said you wanted to be?" That kind of mirror keeps you honest. And it's often the difference between a slow drift and a timely course correction.

There's a pattern I've noticed among leaders who manage to keep their values visible over decades. They build in rhythms of pause. Whether it's a five-minute daily check-in or a more structured monthly reflection, they find ways to step back and look at how they're showing up. Not to feel good about their intentions, but to examine their impact. It's a habit that builds inner alignment. And that alignment creates outer consistency.

Sometimes the challenge isn't in choosing between right and wrong. It's choosing between what's right and what's easy. The honest path rarely comes with applause. It often comes with resistance. But the leaders who stay with it find that what they lose in approval, they gain in trust. And over time, that trust becomes the strongest asset in their leadership.

I've worked with leadership teams that had all the right vision statements written out. But it was always the ones who protected their values when no one was watching who shaped the strongest cultures. Values don't live in documents. They live in decisions. They live in the moments when no one else will know what you chose, but you will.

And once that's lost, rebuilding it takes more than time. It takes truth.

This is not about perfection. Every leader will miss the mark at times. The question is not whether you will fall short. The question is whether you'll have the awareness to recognize it, the courage to admit it, and the humility to course-correct without getting defensive.

Staying true to your mission and values over time doesn't mean standing still. It means moving forward without losing yourself in the process. It means knowing which voice to listen to when everything around you is asking you to adjust your standard.

Leadership without values is noise. It may sound powerful. But it doesn't last.

The leaders who outlast the pressure, who build teams that carry their work forward long after they're gone, are the ones who know what they stand for and, more importantly, who stand for it even when it costs them something.

The Challenges of Sustaining Leadership Balance

Staying true to your values is one thing. Staying true when pressure builds, when the silence in the room grows heavier, or when the cost starts getting personal, that's a different conversation.

Most leaders can explain what they believe. Many speak confidently about the values they stand for. But when things get messy, when timelines are squeezed and the spotlight narrows, clarity begins to fade. What once felt obvious now feels complicated. What used to be a firm line starts to blur.

In my years of working with leaders across different domains and countries, I've seen this play out more often than people expect.

Compromise rarely walks in wearing a name tag. It arrives in small steps. An expense was manipulated to avoid questions. A process was skipped because "this time is different." A comment was ignored in a meeting because calling it out might make things awkward. These aren't big headline moments. But they add up. And left unchecked, they shift the center of how a leader operates.

One of the toughest spots to stand is when you feel torn between expectations from above and responsibility toward those you lead. You want to meet the demands of stakeholders, but you also want to protect the people you lead. At times, these two directions pull in opposite ways. In moments like this, leaders often feel cornered. Taking the easier route can feel like survival. Choosing the harder one feels like friction. But that's the space where character is tested. That's where values move from aspiration to evidence.

Doing the right thing does not always come with applause. In fact, it often costs something. Time. Trust. Visibility. I've seen leaders step back from the spotlight because they refused to compromise on their standards. I've seen managers speak up, knowing full well it might come with pushback. These decisions can feel lonely in the moment. But they are remembered. And more often than not, they shape the kind of culture others want to be part of.

On the other hand, I've also seen good people get worn down. Most missteps I've witnessed weren't born out of bad intent. They happened when leaders were tired. When they felt pressure but no support. When they had more questions than answers and no one to turn to. They didn't walk in planning to let things slip. But without clear reinforcement, they chose what was easiest in that moment. And then did it again the next time.

This is why values can't be left to chance. They need structure. The leaders who hold their ground over time tend to build habits that keep them aligned. They reflect regularly. They surround themselves with people who don't sugarcoat things. They write down their personal boundaries and revisit them often. These aren't rituals for show. They're practical tools that give you a foundation when everything around you feels unstable.

One question I've returned to often in my own decision-making is simple. Would I be comfortable if this decision appeared on the front page tomorrow morning with my name next to it? That question resets your lens. It brings the decision into the open and places it in full view. When I ask it honestly, the next step becomes easier to see.

I think of Major Sandeep Unnikrishnan and what he stood for during the 26/11 Mumbai attacks. He led his team from the 51 Special Action Group into the Taj Mahal Palace Hotel, where hostages were trapped and danger was around every corner. One of his commandos, Sunil Kumar Yadav, was critically wounded during the operation. Major Sandeep made sure his teammate was pulled out safely, refusing to leave anyone behind. When the team was pinned down, he chose to move forward alone, knowing exactly what that choice meant.

In a close and brutal firefight, he was shot while shielding others. His last words still echo, *"Do not come up, I will handle them."* That came from a place of deep responsibility. He stepped forward because it was the right thing to do. His leadership was about standing where it mattered most.

What you do when others are watching matters. Teams notice when you take responsibility instead of shifting blame. They remember when you stay transparent even when it's uncomfortable. Most of all, they learn from how you handle the grey areas. They watch how you act when doing the right thing means disappointing someone above you. They notice when you choose clarity over approval. That is what builds trust. And while most decisions in leadership won't carry life-or-death weight, they still leave an imprint. They tell people what you stand for. And more importantly, they tell you what you are willing to carry on your own.

Some of the strongest leaders I've worked with do not try to handle this alone. They build small, trusted circles of reflection. These are not formal review boards. They are quiet conversations with people who understand your values and won't let you forget them. Sometimes it's a colleague, sometimes a coach, sometimes a close peer who has no stake in your decisions. What matters is that they have permission to ask hard questions. And you have the willingness to answer them honestly.

Another habit that makes a real difference is defining your lines early. In the military, these are called Terms of Reference. When preparing for an operation or writing a military appreciation, the very first thing that's laid down is writing down your non-negotiables when things are steady, not in the middle of a crisis. Do it when your head is clear, before the tension starts to build. Because when things go sideways, you won't have time to process new values. You'll fall back on the ones you've identified and rehearsed.

Creating a culture where truth can speak freely doesn't happen by making grand declarations. It happens in small ways. Asking for feedback. Listening without defending. Acting on what you hear. And showing people that telling the truth won't cost them their seat at the table.

Leaders who do this well normalize discomfort. They don't panic when someone raises a concern. They thank them. They respond, not with silence, but with change. Over time, this becomes culture. And culture is what holds when the pressure rises.

When mistakes happen, and they will, the response is what matters most. Owning what happened. Acknowledge the impact. Correct it. Not quietly, but clearly. The longer the delay, the louder the damage. I've seen trust rebuilt after honest failure. I've rarely seen it return after avoidance.

There is a quiet strength in leaders who lead this way. They are not loud. They are not always celebrated. But their teams know what they stand for. And that knowing creates safety.

Leadership is not measured by the absence of mistakes. It is measured by the presence of accountability. It is defined by how often people feel safe telling you the truth, and how often you tell it back.

The leaders who stand the test of time are not the ones who had perfect records. They are the ones who never stopped aligning their actions with their values, even when the cost was high.

They didn't talk about standards. They practiced them, and that's what people remember.

Final Reflection: How Will You Lead and Inspire Moving Forward?

When the applause fades, the targets change, and the room quiets down, the question that remains is this: *How will you lead now?*

Everything you've read up to this point points toward one truth. Leadership isn't defined by how much you know or how many people report to you. It's defined by how you show up when there is no script. It's measured by what you're willing to hold on to, especially when letting go would be easier.

I've worked with leaders who had every metric working in their favor. They were liked, promoted, and high-performing. But when pressure rose, their decisions cracked their credibility. Not because they weren't skilled, but because they hadn't clarified what they stood for. And when you haven't done that work, circumstances do it for you. They shape you, instead of you shaping them.

I've also seen the opposite. Leaders who had little formal power, no titles of significance, and minimal visibility. But they led with clarity. They made hard calls with quiet conviction. And the people around them trusted them without needing a reason every time. Because over time, their values spoke louder than their position ever could.

So the question I leave you with is simple. What kind of leader are you becoming?

This isn't a branding exercise. It's not a leadership model or a personal pitch. It's a real audit. What kind of impact are you making when no one is measuring? What kind of environment are you shaping without even realizing it?

Inspirational Leadership isn't a badge or a trait. It's a pattern. It shows up in how you treat people who have nothing to offer you. It lives in how you respond when feedback catches you off guard. It shows up in how you act when telling the truth makes things harder, not easier. These aren't small things. They build the emotional environment that others work in every day.

One of the things I've encouraged in every team I've worked with is to build a clear standard for decision-making. Not a list of policies. A filter. A way to test your choices. Would you be okay explaining this decision to someone you deeply respect? Would you be proud if your team repeated it tomorrow in your absence? These are not difficult questions to ask. But they require honesty, which most people avoid.

Now think about how you're carrying the Four Cornerstones.

Is your passion still visible to the people who follow you? Or have you replaced it with performance targets and productivity charts?

Are your people still central to how you lead? Or have they become names on a tracker, updates in a dashboard, metrics to manage?

Is your performance driven by clarity and discipline? Or are you constantly switching gears based on what's trending or what's convenient?

And what about your legacy? Are you building something others can carry forward, or are you building something that ends with you?

If your answers are uncomfortable, that's a good sign. That means you're paying attention. Most leaders don't fail because they lack knowledge. They fail because they stop checking in with themselves. They stop asking whether their current pace, tone, and decisions still reflect who they said they wanted to be.

There's no perfect way to lead. But there is a consistent one. When your actions reflect your commitments, your leadership begins to build momentum. People around you don't need explanations. They already know what to expect from you. And that consistency is what creates trust.

If you've led long enough, you've likely already made decisions you regret. That's normal. The goal here is not flawlessness. It's alignment. If you've drifted, get back on track. If you've stayed steady, double down. What matters is that you're intentional now.

So, how will you lead moving forward?

With more presence? With more honesty? With more clarity on where you won't bend, and with more courage to walk away from what no longer fits?

The decisions ahead will test you. Some will be loud. Others will happen in quiet corners. Either way, they'll leave a mark. And you'll either carry that mark with pride, or you'll spend your energy trying to hide it.

Choose the kind of leadership that doesn't need a badge. Choose the kind that holds up even when no one's watching. Choose the kind that leaves people better, not drained. The kind that listens more than it explains. And above all, the kind that lives by the values it claims to respect.

Because how you lead from this point forward won't be judged by what you say. It will be shaped by what you consistently do.

Personal Leadership Commitment Exercise

This is not a checklist. This is where intention meets decision. Where your values step outside of theory and begin to shape your behavior with clarity.

These three exercises are designed to help you stop, reflect, and reset before the next choice tests your alignment. Leadership built on these four cornerstones doesn't happen overnight. It happens through steady, conscious choices.

1. The No-Deal Decision

Think of one ethical line you won't cross. Now write one realistic situation where crossing that line would benefit you directly.

Example:

"I will never shift blame onto my team. Even if taking the fall damages how I'm perceived."

This is your "no-deal" moment, the one you commit to walk away from, regardless of what's at stake.

Now ask:

What will help me stand by this when the time comes?

Who do I trust enough to remind me of this if I start drifting?

2. The Pressure Filter

Write down three situations where your leadership might be tested in the next 90 days. Think of things that are likely, not extreme.

Examples:

- Delivering disappointing news to a senior stakeholder.

- Holding a high-performing team member accountable.

- Speaking up in a room where everyone agrees with the wrong thing.

Now write one action for each scenario that would reflect your values, not your fear.

Ask yourself:

Am I willing to protect my standard when the cost is not hypothetical?

3. The Personal Debrief

At the end of the next two weeks, ask yourself this:

- Did I avoid a hard conversation when I should have leaned in?

- Did I make a decision I'm proud of, not because of how it looked, but because of how it felt?

- Did I carry myself in a way that someone else could quietly model?

Write down your answers. Keep them private. The goal here is not approval. It's awareness.

Clarity builds through repetition. And the more often you ask these questions, the harder it becomes to lead out of alignment.

The Mark You Leave

Some forms of leadership stay with people long after the moment has passed. They don't rely on recognition. They don't need attention to feel steady. They show up in consistent decisions, especially when the pressure makes it easier to shift course.

You don't build this kind of leadership through a title. It takes shape through how you carry your responsibility when no one is watching. And people notice. Maybe not always in the moment, but the impression lasts.

The principle I've carried with me through every season is simple. People First, Mission Always. That line has held me in tough calls and quiet ones. It's helped me choose clarity when comfort felt more appealing. It reminded me that trust, once earned through action, can carry more weight than any applause.

Leadership that stays doesn't need explanation. It doesn't try to prove its value. You'll find it in the steady tone a leader holds under stress. In the quiet confidence of someone who's not chasing credit. And in the way people begin to carry themselves differently because they were led by someone who made space for them to grow.

Let that be your standard.

<u>Key Takeaways</u>

- **Leadership that inspires is built on balance:** The most trusted leaders are those who hold Passion, People, Performance, and Legacy together, adjusting when one pulls too far, realigning when something starts to slip.

- **Presence matters more than position:** What people remember isn't the title you held, but how you made them feel when things were unclear, how you showed up when it was easier to step back, and how you responded when no one was watching.

- **Passion fuels your purpose,** but it must be tied to clarity, reinforced with rhythm, and grounded in what truly matters to those you lead.

- **People are your true leadership measure:** Metrics can measure progress, but people measure trust. Your influence lives in how you are seen, supported, and valued by your people.

- **Performance thrives in rhythm, not pressure:** Strong leaders don't drive teams with force. They create environments where expectations are clear, feedback is real, and rhythm builds ownership.

- **Legacy starts now, not later:** It's not what follows you, it's what continues through others because of how you led today. Your legacy is built decision by decision, especially in the quiet moments.

- **Your values need reinforcement, not reminders:** Clarity comes from preparation. Structure, habits, and honest feedback circles protect your alignment when things get hard.

- **Consistency beats charisma:** What earns trust isn't style, it's showing up the same way in every room, holding the same authentic standard whether praised, pushed, or questioned.

- **Integrity holds when preparation leads:** Leaders who've defined their non-negotiables in calm seasons respond with strength in chaos. When values are clear, the response becomes instinctive.

- **Leadership that endures is lived, not stated:** Whether it's in daily choices or high-stakes moments like that of Major Sandeep Unnikrishnan, true leadership is revealed through what you're willing to carry, protect, and stand for, even when it costs you something.

Conclusion: Living the Four Cornerstones Every Day: The Leadership Journey Never Ends

There comes a point in every leader's journey where knowledge is no longer the issue. The issue is consistency.

Most leaders I've worked with aren't lacking frameworks. What they need is a way to keep the right things at the center when pressure, pace, and politics start pulling them in different directions. That's where the Four Cornerstones come in.

What started for me as patterns, such as the things I noticed across units, across countries, across cultures, eventually became structure. Passion, People, Performance, and Legacy weren't boxes to tick. They were signals. When things were working, all four were present. When things were off, at least one was neglected.

The leaders who sustain impact over time are not the ones who rotate between these elements based on what's urgent. They build the ability to carry them together.

When a leader speaks with clarity and purpose, people respond. When that same leader listens without losing standards, teams align. When those teams execute with discipline and ownership, results follow. And when those results are anchored in values, not pressure, they leave behind more than metrics. They leave behind a culture.

I've seen this across all kinds of leadership transitions. Sometimes it was a founder stepping away from the company they built and preparing someone else to take the lead. The founders who did this well stayed close enough to guide, but far enough to let the new leader stand on their own. Sometimes it was a senior officer handing over command during high-stakes operations. The officers who led these transitions were well-focused on setting the tone before they left, making sure the team had clear direction, strong confidence, and trust in the new leader from the very first step. They understood that how they handed over leadership mattered as much as how they had carried it. And sometimes it was a new executive taking charge of a team that had been worn down by poor leadership. The executive who turned it around didn't start with bold plans; they started with restoring belief in the mission, in the work, and in each other. They listened before leading, earned trust before setting targets, and helped the team feel seen again.

In every one of these transitions, the leaders who made the biggest impact were defined by how they showed up rather than what they knew. They made sure their passion was still visible. They made space for people. They kept performance accountable without making it mechanical. And they carried themselves with a sense of duty that extended beyond their role.

That's what integration looks like. It's not visible in your calendar. It's felt in your presence. It's sensed in how people behave around you. Whether they speak honestly. Whether they take initiative. Whether they trust your silence as much as your speech.

No single quality will carry a leader through every situation. But the combination of these four, when lived intentionally, creates a foundation that can adapt across environments.

You can be firm without being distant when your passion and people stay aligned.

You can demand excellence without micromanaging when performance is built on trust.

You can build systems that last when your leadership isn't tied to your position.

The Four Cornerstones are signs that tell you how your leadership is doing. If one of them is being ignored, that's probably where something needs your attention. If one of them is taking up all your focus, it may be causing problems with the others. When something feels off, check which of the four you've stopped paying attention to, or which one has taken over everything else.

If leadership is a journey, and not a moment, then you need a structure that moves with you. Something that doesn't fade when circumstances change. Something that speaks louder than your title. Something that stays.

That's what these four elements give you. They give you something real to return to, no matter the room you're in.

The leaders I respect most don't talk about these principles often. They embody them. You see it in their tone. Their presence. Their decisions. You feel it when you walk into a room they've shaped. It's quieter than charisma, but it runs deeper. And it outlasts them.

So don't use these pillars as reminders. Use them as checks. Use them to ask yourself:

- *Am I still leading with clear intent, or am I just going through the motions?*

- *Am I making it easier for people to grow, or getting in the way?*

- *Is the way I perform something I'd be proud to see repeated by others?*

- *And if I were to leave tomorrow, what would stay behind?*

Those questions are not for performance reviews. They're for your own reflection. Ask them often enough, and you won't need to memorize the Four Cornerstones. You'll become someone who carries them without thinking.

That's when leadership stops being reactive and starts becoming real.

Final Words of Wisdom on Leadership

Leadership isn't a title you earn. It's a responsibility you carry.

And the longer you carry it, the more you realize that it's not meant to serve you. It's meant to serve others. Your team. Your mission. The values you claim to stand for.

The leaders who have left the strongest impression on me weren't always the ones with the loudest presence. They were the ones who led with a clear sense of purpose. They didn't need to be followed. They needed to be trusted. And they earned that trust not by being perfect, but by being consistent.

They didn't chase visibility. They stood by their people. They didn't manage from above. They stayed at work. They made space for conversations no one else wanted to have. They told the truth when it was easier to stay quiet. And they never used pressure as a reason to lower the standard.

What I learned over the years is this: leadership begins to matter most when things are at their messiest. When clarity is in short supply. When decisions come with weight. When people are tired and waiting for someone to hold the line.

In those moments, your influence doesn't come from your authority. It comes from who you are when nothing else is holding you up.

True leadership is not about being right. It's about staying responsible. For your choices. For your presence. For the example you set.

And that's where your values start to show. Not in big moments, but in the quiet ways you carry yourself. It shows up in how you correct someone without tearing them down. In how you speak up for someone who isn't in the room to speak for themselves. In how you make space for feedback that's hard to hear but still important.

That kind of leadership builds something worth following. Something that doesn't rely on power to move people. Something that earns influence through integrity, not position.

And it lasts. Because people may forget your projects, your plans, and even your wins. But they will remember how they felt under your leadership.

They will remember whether you made them feel valuable or invisible. Whether you gave them space to grow or pushed them aside when it didn't suit you. Whether you modeled courage or expected it from others without showing it yourself.

The real test is simple. Could someone who watched you lead walk into their own leadership role with more clarity, more care, and more conviction?

If yes, then you've already done the work. If not, there's still time to start.

What stays with me, and what I leave with you, is what's stayed true through every phase of my life: People First, Mission Always. That phrase has helped me find my bearings in rooms where values were missing. It reminded me to stay present when performance was easier to prioritize than people. And it kept me grounded when legacy felt like a long way off.

Lead in a way that no one has to wonder where you stand.

Lead in a way that your values are always clear, even when you say nothing.

Lead in a way that you don't have to explain.

Because when leadership becomes service, trust becomes natural. And trust is where the real change begins.

A Call to Action: Becoming the Leader the World Needs

We've covered the framework. You've seen how passion, people, performance, and legacy aren't leadership theories, they're tests. And you've seen what it takes to hold them when the pressure rises.

The next step is not about learning more. It's about choosing how you lead from this point on.

Leadership doesn't need more slogans. It needs substance. Not promises. Presence.

Right now, the world is filled with people who are uncertain who to follow. They're not waiting for someone flawless. They're waiting for someone steady. Someone who says what needs to be said, even when it costs them. Someone who protects their people before they protect their image. Someone who knows how to stand still when everyone else is reacting.

This kind of leadership doesn't start in a seminar. It starts when you stop trying to look like a leader and start acting like one in the small, daily moments that count.

It begins when you stop letting pressure lower your standard. When you make the harder call because it protects trust. When you stay patient with someone who's struggling, even when it slows you down. When you raise someone else's voice before your own.

Leaders are not defined by the title they carry. They're defined by what others begin to believe is possible because of the way they lead.

So here's the call.

Start with your circle. Lead it with clarity and care. Lead it like your presence matters. Because it does.

Don't wait to be asked. Look around. Someone near you is watching how you lead. Whether you mentor them formally or not, you're shaping their view of what leadership looks like. Every decision you make is a blueprint for someone else's behavior.

You don't need a plan for the next decade. You need to move with intention in the next decision.

- Choose passion when giving up feels easier.

- Choose people when it would be faster to focus only on the task.

- Choose disciplined execution, even when shortcuts are available.

- And choose legacy every time you're tempted to protect your own comfort.

Mentor someone, even if informally. Ask them what kind of leader they want to be, and then help them become it. Share your mistakes. Let them see the whole story. The next generation of leaders isn't looking for a perfect model. They're looking for someone real enough to learn from.

And stay a student yourself. Leadership doesn't finish. It deepens. Stay hungry to get better. Stay curious about how others lead with a strength you admire. Stay open to being questioned. Growth doesn't weaken you. It sharpens you.

And finally, keep this phrase close: People First, Mission Always. It's simple enough to remember when things get chaotic. And strong enough to hold you when the lines blur. The world doesn't need louder leaders. It needs steadier ones.

Be one of them.

Next Steps for Readers: Practical Applications and Further Development

Leadership doesn't end at clarity. It begins there.

Reading alone will not change how you lead. Practice will. Repetition will. Honest reflection will.

So here are your next steps. Not as a checklist, but as a living rhythm. A way to apply what you've absorbed, and to keep building what you've started.

1. Carry the Four Cornerstones Into Your Routine

These four cornerstones, Passion, People, Performance, and Legacy, are not categories. They are conditions. When they're strong, your leadership holds. When one of them weakens, things start to drift.

Start each week with one simple prompt:

- What will I do this week to live my passion with clarity?

- Who needs me to show up with attention and care, not just results?

- What standard must be reinforced, not assumed?

- And what quiet decision will contribute to the culture I leave behind?

Write the answers. Act on them. Review them. Let the repetition shape your rhythm.

2. Mentor One Leader Behind You

Don't wait for formal programs. You don't need a title to guide someone else's growth. You need intent.

Think of someone in your team, your network, your orbit, someone with potential but without a clear mirror. Give them your time. Not your advice. Your time.

Ask them what they value. Ask them what kind of leader they want to be. Then share where you've struggled. What did you get wrong? What you still wrestle with.

Because the next generation of leaders doesn't need heroes. They need real models who are still learning.

3. Audit Yourself in Private

Every 30 days, take 20 minutes to ask:

- Did I hold back from being direct to keep things comfortable?

- Have I said yes to something I wasn't proud of?

- Have I failed to correct something I knew was wrong?

- Have I lived People First, Mission Always, or have I slipped into self-preservation?

You don't need to show these answers to anyone. But they should shape the decisions you make next.

4. Keep Learning, but Filter the Noise

There's no shortage of leadership material. What there is a shortage of is self-awareness. Pick a mentor. Pick one course or program a year that stretches your thinking. Read something that provokes you to think differently.

But more than that, pay attention to how you lead when no one's watching. That data will teach you more than any certification.

5. Build a Long-Term Map With Short-Term Honesty

Think in quarters, not decades. Map the four cornerstones to how you lead in your current role.

Ask:

- Where am I most consistent?

- Where am I faking it?

- Where is my team carrying me instead of growing through me?

Then commit to one change per quarter. That's it. One. Build it into your behavior until it becomes natural. Then move to the next.

This is how leaders grow: by letting inspiration set the direction and consistency do the work.

Appendices & Additional Resources

These tools are designed to help you apply the Four Cornerstones to your current context, at your own pace. Use them as reflection prompts, development checkpoints, or team conversation starters. No jargon. No filler. Only what helps you lead better.

Appendix A: Leadership Self-Assessment Worksheets

Use these questions to evaluate where you are today across each of the Four Cornerstones. Answer honestly. These are not performance reviews. They're clarity check-ins.

PASSION CHECK

- Do I still believe in the purpose behind what I lead?

- Am I showing up with energy, or just going through the motions?

- What drains my passion right now, and what fuels it?

PEOPLE CHECK

- When was the last time I asked someone, "What do you need to succeed?"

- Do people feel supported by my presence, or only directed by my authority?

- What is it like to be led by me when things are uncertain?

PERFORMANCE CHECK

- Are my expectations clear, or assumed?

- Does my team know how success is measured and why?

- What system am I relying on to make sure we stay mission-ready?

LEGACY CHECK

- What values do I want my team to carry after I leave?

- What behaviors am I reinforcing, knowingly or unknowingly?

- If I stepped away today, what would remain?

Appendix B: Personal Leadership Planning Templates

These planning templates are built for rhythm, not rigidity. Use them quarterly or monthly. The goal is not to predict, but to prepare.

Leadership Clarity Card (Complete Once Every Quarter)

- What personal value holds your leadership together, no matter the setting? ________________________________

- My 3 Leadership Priorities This Quarter:

    1. ____

    2. ____

    3. ____

- What I Will Stop Doing: ______________________________

- What I Will Continue or Start Doing to Lead Better:

    ____

- Who Will I Mentor/Coach: ______________________________

- One Thing I Will Do to Live People First, Mission Always:

    ____

Weekly Leadership Rhythm (5-Minute Monday Check-In)

- What decision this week will test my integrity?

- Who needs more presence than direction from me?

- What standard needs to be reinforced quietly?

- How will I live my legacy in real time this week?

Appendix C: Recommended Readings & Case Studies

Personal Picks to Strengthen Each Cornerstone

This list isn't academic. It's practical. These books and stories reflect what I've seen matter most when you're leading real people, under real pressure, with real consequences. Some are familiar names, others might surprise you. They've stayed with me, and I believe they'll add value to how you lead through Passion, People, Performance, and Legacy.

PASSION – The Reason You Keep Showing Up

When your work starts to feel like a weight, not a purpose, these books help you find your footing again. And the people mentioned here didn't treat passion like a mood. They built entire careers around staying connected to what matters.

What to read:

- Start with Why by Simon Sinek – Focus on how purpose fuels passion.

- Drive: The Surprising Truth About What Motivates Us by Daniel H. Pink – Explores intrinsic motivation as a passion driver.

- Awaken the Giant Within by Tony Robbins – On reigniting personal passion and purpose.

- Grit by Angela Duckworth – Passion sustained over time through perseverance.

- The Element by Sir Ken Robinson – Finding the point where natural talent meets personal passion.

People who lived it:

- Elon Musk (SpaceX, Tesla) – Passion for innovation and human evolution.

- Howard Schultz (Starbucks) – Passion for creating a "third place" beyond home and work.

- Dr. A.P.J. Abdul Kalam – Passion for science, education, and youth empowerment in India.

PEOPLE – How You Treat the Ones Who Trust You

Leadership gets real when people stop seeing you as a boss and start trusting you as someone who won't fail them. These books sharpen your ability to lead with care, and these case studies show what happens when empathy is part of the standard.

What to read:

- Leaders Eat Last by Simon Sinek – The biology of trust and empathy in team leadership.

- The Five Dysfunctions of a Team by Patrick Lencioni – Insights on trust and collaboration.

- Primal Leadership by Daniel Goleman, Richard Boyatzis – Emotional intelligence and resonant leadership.

- Multipliers by Liz Wiseman – How leaders get more from their people.

- Everybody Matters by Bob Chapman & Raj Sisodia – Leading with heart and putting people first.

People who lived it:

- Satya Nadella (Microsoft) – Cultural transformation through empathy and inclusiveness.

- Jacinda Ardern (Former PM of New Zealand) – Empathy-based leadership in times of crisis.

- The Tata Group (India) – A people-first legacy built on trust and ethics.

PERFORMANCE – The Work That Speaks for Itself

What you believe as a leader only becomes real when it shows up in what you deliver, day after day, under pressure. These books bring structure to that side of the role. The people highlighted here showed how high standards and consistent results don't need drama; they need rhythm.

What to read:

- Good to Great by Jim Collins – Why some companies (and leaders) leap to great performance.

- Execution: The Discipline of Getting Things Done by Larry Bossidy & Ram Charan – Leadership and performance linkage.

- Measure What Matters by John Doerr – OKRs and performance tracking.

- The High Potential Leader by Ram Charan – From performance to leadership excellence.

- Extreme Ownership by Jocko Willink & Leif Babin – Military-inspired performance and accountability.

People who lived it:

- Indra Nooyi (PepsiCo) – Performance driven by strategic vision and inclusive leadership.

- Toyota Production System (Lean Manufacturing) – High performance through systems thinking.

- Apple under Steve Jobs – Focused innovation and world-class execution.

LEGACY – What You Leave Behind Without Saying a Word

Legacy isn't what people say when you retire. It's how they act when you're not around. These books and stories highlight the kind of leadership that doesn't end when the title does.

What to read:

- Legacy by James Kerr – Lessons from the rugby team on building enduring legacies.

- True North by Bill George – Leading with authenticity and leaving a legacy of integrity.

- The 7 Habits of Highly Effective People by Stephen R. Covey – Principles-based legacy creation.

- What Got You Here Won't Get You There by Marshall Goldsmith – Behavioral legacy and leadership evolution.

- Die Empty by Todd Henry – Living fully and leaving nothing undone.

People who lived it:

- Nelson Mandela – Legacy of reconciliation and visionary transformation.

- Ratan Tata – Building an ethical legacy and social impact.

- The Rockefeller Foundation – Philanthropic legacy with global impact.